In the Home of the Famous Dead

In the Home of the Famous Dead

COLLECTED POEMS

Jo McDougall

Foreword by Carl Adamshick

THE UNIVERSITY OF ARKANSAS PRESS
FAYETTEVILLE
2015

5-9-17

For Sam Hazo

and

for Rita

My circus animals were all on show,
Those stilted boys, that burnished chariot,
Lion and woman and the Lord knows what.
                                   —W. B. Yeats

CONTENTS

Towns Facing Railroads

From Darkening Porches
1996

Dirt

Satisfied with Havoc
2004

Under an Arkansas Sky
CHAPBOOK
2010

FOREWORD

Jo McDougall loves you. It's why she has written the five full-length poetry collections contained in this book. She writes about you and how you think. She never posits herself a god or speaks from beyond the grave, although ghosts have a certain residency in her pages. Her art is sunk in the real. I write "real" and immediately want to clarify by writing "truthful." But then I think neither of those words is a helpful expression, and then feel "honesty" is the right word. But really that doesn't help either; all the big words cause trouble, or seem like argument starters. What Jo does is portray the living with a calculating neighborly eye. Her art is an art of gossip, of keeping tabs, of how we talk to others after long bouts of thinking.

Jo's had a fairly steady stream of publications. From 1983 (a hefty chapbook, *Women Who Marry Houses*, Coyote Love Press) to 2004, not more than five years passed before you could find a new collection. Born in Arkansas, she was in her forties when her publishing career started, but it's important to remember she was urgently reading and writing in the late 1950s, when the poetic landscape was different and had, in lots of ways, a smaller population with heavier black lines dividing camps on poetry's map; that's the era in which this poet raised on a rice farm in the South learned her trade.

I like to think of this book as a city, many of its occupants home doing daily things—sitting on the stoop with coffee or folding laundry, getting ready or just arriving home from work and thinking about themselves and others—but the book is a string of small, unincorporated towns with neighbors and strangers all keeping their proper distance. And Jo is an elected official, a sort of emotional tax collector entrusted to tell their stories. Her manifesto, if she has one, is inward and quiet, the rules and edicts all her own. Jo's more a psychologist or psychoanalyst interpreting image and symbol than a philosopher shuffling rhetoric and logic as if they were a worn red deck.

When I read McDougall I'm reminded words aren't so powerful on their own. They need to be harnessed to other words. They need to move and circle around and to communicate with one another and form a vortex, a dynamo. Words are pack animals. They do best moving as a collective. I love to see Jo control the pack. I love it when life is elevated into the realm of art. Jo McDougall is exacting, everything needs to be right, and she makes it that way.

—Carl Adamshick

ACKNOWLEDGMENTS

Thank you to the following presses for granting permission to reprint the books in this collection: BkMk Press (*The Woman in the Next Booth*), Autumn House Press (*Dirt* and *Satisfied with Havoc*), and Tavern Books (*Under an Arkansas Sky*). The books *Towns Facing Railroads* and *From Darkening Porches* (University of Arkansas Press) and *Women Who Marry Houses* (Coyote Love Press) also appear in the collection. Thanks to artist Michael Sowa for permission to use *A Summer Night's Melancholy*. A special thanks to BkMk Press and Tavern Books for their generous support of this project.

I'm grateful to Sam Hazo, Miller Williams, Carl Adamshick, and Tom Lavoie, early champions of this collection; to Stephen Meats, William Trowbridge, and Maryfrances Wagner for invaluable editing; to Chris Purcell, Alarie Tennille, and Carol Sickman-Garner for incisive proofreading; to Alice Friman, Matthew Dickman, Beth Brubaker, David Baker, and Jeanie Wilson for heartening encouragement and support; and to my editors at the University of Arkansas Press, Mike Bieker, Melissa King, and Brian King. Thanks to Carl Adamshick for his thoughtful foreword. And a special thank you goes to my husband, Charles, for all the support through all the years.

Many of the poems in this collection, some in different versions, first appeared in the following publications: *Arkansas Democrat-Gazette, Arkansas Literary Forum, Arkansas Review, Arkansas Times, Bitterroot, Chimerical, Controlled Burn, Cow Creek Review, Georgia Review, Intro 13, Jumping Pond: Poems & Stories from the Ozarks, Kansas Voices, Little Balkans Review, Louisiana Literature, Maine Times, Men and Women: Together and Alone, Midwest Quarterly, Morning News, Natural Bridge, New Century North American Poets, New Letters, New Mexico Humanities Review, New Orleans Review, Nimrod, North American Review, Ohio State University Journal, Paragraph, Pebble Lake Review, Perihelion, Poetry East, Poetry Miscellany, Quarterly, Review, Rio Grande Review, Roots* and Recognition: *Where Poetry Comes From, Salamander, Skirt, Slow Dancer, Southern Poetry Review, Texas Review, Today's Alternative News, Tortilla,* and *White River Literary Arena.*

Thanks to the editors of the *Hudson Review,* in which "Threads" first appeared, and to the editors of the *Kenyon Review,* in which "What We Need" first appeared.

Many of the poems in this collection were written in the time afforded me by the generosity of the Arkansas Arts Council, Pittsburg State University, the MacDowell Colony, and the DeWitt Wallace/Reader's Digest foundation.

from Women Who Marry Houses

CHAPBOOK

1983

On a Sunday Night in Hattiesburg

A man clicks an index open
to a certain address in Baltimore.
A woman half as tall as a thumbnail
hops out.
Mistaking her for a silverfish,
he scoots her off the desk.
He learns the next day
his friend has died in Baltimore,
a woman whose husband is charged
with killing his wife.
The husband swears that she died in her sleep
that she cried out once
that bruises on her body
came from inside
came from the broken bones.

The Displaced

He sat on my bed.
He lit a cigarette.
I said Excuse me but how did you get in?
He said through the mail slot
and where did I keep the scotch?

The next morning
he came back with a china suitcase—white,
the state of Maine emblazoned with roses.
That was all in 1965.
Today I promised
I would call him Al.

Alice B. Toklas and Moon: A Letter to Gertrude

It was anger with you at some slight
made me stomp out to the garden
to look at the moon half-sitting on our house.
The night felt like fine porcelain
left standing in cool windows.
I examined the moon from behind.
I got round the other side.
I got on the moon and rode.

I could hear you calling Alice Alice
as the moon rose.
Don't worry; I'm fine. I'm waited on
by long, soft girls.
I have a garden of my own.
I've worked out the colors as you do words:
green upon green
and the shock of one red canna.

My peonies bloom large as plates.
(Don't forget you've invited twelve for Sunday next.)
This week I'll send you asters
just the color for the hall,
and in the fall I'll send you the seed of the canna,
microscopic, prolific,
black as Sunday shoes.

The Woman in the Next Booth

1987

Walking Down Prospect

I walk down Prospect
behind the building with the Gothic windows.
Inside me your names fly up like two quail.
When they are gone
I pull my coat around me.
When I get home
I try to call you.
Where you are in the world now it is dark.
The phone rings into that.

Labor Day

The boy's mother hears it on the radio.
A fishing boat has been found.
She walks through the house,
reassuring the backs of chairs.

Her husband comes home from the lake.
Dusk filters through the screen.
Sit down, he says.
He puts his hat on the table.

The Black and Small Birds of Remorse

come in the cool hours
one by one
to perch on the backs of chairs.
Anywhere you are trying to start over—
tossing green salad, changing white sheets—
they glide in of a sudden,
shift from foot to foot.

Silly Women

When death sees a silly woman
he ambles over
and asks her to dance.
If she says Thank you no
he puts his hand on her shoulder anyway
turns her around
teaches her an old step
or two.

Death likes silly women
who believe the names he gives them
who will be ready when he wants to go
who dance a little closer than they should.

Settlement

They had a house.
They had her mother's mantel clock
and his grandfather's bed.
When he left he took nothing belonging to him.
He has been gone a long time.
Today a letter comes.
He will sell her the rocker she gave him one Christmas,
and the bed.
She responds.
She will sell him the mantel clock.
She is careful to say
she has had the clock repaired.
It keeps better time.

Women Who Marry Houses

have lost husbands
to time or to other women.
They look for smaller houses
with hipped roofs.
They move into neighborhoods with large trees.
Women who marry houses
are fond of the dark
when the house cracks its knuckles.

Act

Toward the last my aunt writes
all the hymns she knows
on little slips of paper
and tapes them onto the lampshade
beside her bed.
She says she does this to test her mind.
It makes the light dim.

The 875

In Gillett, a town in Arkansas,
on January twelfth of every year
eight hundred and seventy-five citizens
buy tickets for platters of raccoon and rice.

Trappers bring the coons in, skinned,
the legs gone except for one
ending in the little hand
to make certain that no dog
or cat has been run in.

A Lady Charged with Involuntary Manslaughter Says

it will go bad
but you won't know when.
Say some night,
driving fast along the flats of Kansas,
not too fast,
thinking back:
    You were
    brushing your hair,
    taking off your clothes,
    pouring a scotch

The car takes a hill, reaches the top.
Something there, maybe not,
the shadow of a cloud, cast by the moonlight,
or something in your headlights, kneeling.

Men

She waits in the car and watches two men
try to sell a truck
to the man who brought her here.
He slams the truck's good door
and lifts the hood.
The men talk,
looking at the ground
as though they were reading something there.
She leans back in the car,
glad to be in the company of men.

The Bessemer

We called the building
my father housed the Bessemer in
the pumping shed.
Loretta and Horace
lived in the lean-to beside the shed
so that Horace could listen for
a shift in the Bessemer's sound.
He had to keep it running, day and night,
to water my father's rice fields.

Because of the noise it made in the lean-to,
nobody could talk.
When Loretta set the table for supper,
vibration from the engine
wrinkled the milk.

One morning Loretta went into a part of the shed
where Horace had told her not to go.
Her sleeve was caught
in the belt of the Bessemer. Or so
we suppose. Horace found her.
Over the noise
nobody heard her when she screamed.

Harlot Hag Dry Harpy

A woman from Opelousas
came to live
with a barker from Royal American Shows
who had lived with an alligator lady, and Siamese twins.
So the woman from Opelousas
would sometimes paint a harelip on herself,
tape down an eyelid, paint her nose black, sleep on all fours.
Once she tied her ankle to her thigh
and hopped over to him and did his will.

On those nights he could go on forever.
On those nights he'd chant a crawling song,
Pomegranate sequin dove my harlot hag dry harpy,
as he would cradle her head against his face
he'd painted purple
for her
and he would cry.
She'd lick his tears, he'd rock her:
Jesus Mother Mary Martha Tessie Christ Lord Love

The Professor of Chinese Dialects in a Small University Town in Ohio

hears the 5:15 from Akron
slide toward the single strip
of the tiny airport.
Standing at the kitchen table
he makes himself one drink,
unfolds and folds his paper.
After supper his wife goes into the bedroom
goes naked to bed
goes slowly to sleep.

The man sits in the next room, translating Li Po.
He does not see the moon that Li Po speaks of
or the woman.
Under the eaves the night birds
rustle like taffeta.

Something, Anything

The way Mrs. Jensen slams the window shut
in the apartment above says
I'm alive.
Also
Krebbs at the bench on Maple and Third
shows off his new teeth.
Irma Bailey is swiping a dirty menu
from the Café Royale
to show to Mrs. Payton who's never been there.

Pilgrims, we may not make it.

Reporting Back

There has been an accident.
A bridge has collapsed. The water under it
has taken a bus, a car, a truck.
For days we watch a picture
of the one survivor
who fell with his truck tucked around him, two hundred feet,
to bounce off a passing freighter.
The man will not talk with reporters
or answer his phone.

Some who see what they see will never tell
say they don't remember
say what somebody said they said.
Buy this man a drink.
Ask him
What did you think of going down?
Hydrangeas? Your mother? A fox?
"A fox," he says.

One Mile Out of New Smyrna

you begin to see signs.
A dog crosses the road.
A turtle touches the pavement
and turns back.
A truck with a loose tarp passes;
the tarp reaches out.

The next morning you wake up afraid.

At the Vietnam War Memorial for the American Dead

she finds her son's name.
He comes toward her and grins.
She sees him
step out onto the driveway by the house,
dribble a basketball,
make three perfect hook shots
into the goal his father helped him hang.
She had forgotten how big his hands were.

Silence rocks through her like a train.

The Bluebird Café

Eating alone
I shuffle a magazine
turn the coffee cup
light a cigarette.
There is no one here except for one
waitress, a cook I can't see,
me, and one old woman in a booth.
Why didn't you come home last night?

Before the Doctor Says What He Has to Say

My sister and I go into the room
where our mother is dying.
She will not turn her face from the window.
She gestures as if there is someone she knows
on the hospital lawn.
We realize
we no longer come first in her life.

Before the doctor says what he has to say
we believe she is merely distant,
that we can reach to pull her back
the way as children we waded to our small boat
anchored in the shallows,
rocking and waiting for us.

In the Visitors' Room

In the visitors' room
of a Georgia institution
a woman talks to a man
who pretends to sleep or pretends to listen.
Upstairs
someone is running a vacuum cleaner
back and forth.

The Voice of the Radio Announcer

invites us to tea
wears white gloves
opens an ivory envelope:
 A Camden man was drowned early this morning
 The dismembered body of a Huntsville woman
 was found in the rental lockers
 at a downtown station

The voice gets into a black car
signals to the driver
slides the glass closed

Works

A sharecropper's wife
says her gratitude politely
to the Methodist woman
who brings canned goods and bread
in a Safeway sack.
When the woman leaves,
the wife slams the door, startling
two pictures on the wall.

The Menial

Each woman keeps another woman—
old, painted, with spittle on her chin—
who comes through a small gate when we call her
to cook, to clean our teeth
to suckle our young
even to bed down in our names
to make love in our names
to have our children.

She will do almost anything except
dig in the ground a rectangle
sink into that a box with a lid
climb into that naked.

Things That Will Keep

On my father's desk sits a 1920s vase
in the shape of Loie Fuller, dancing,
and a picture of my mother
smiling from some town nobody remembers.
My father likes to tell
how she bought the vase with egg money
in the Great Depression
and a set of books for me.
They had blue spines.

Today, the morning of her funeral,
it is winter and my mother wears a sensible dress.
Women come into her kitchen
bearing casseroles, molded salads,
things that will keep.
Behind each visitor
my father shuts and shuts the door.

O summer of backyards and sparrows
RedRoverComeOver
O dark after cicadas
that brought my mother watchful to the screen.

Winter Room

The room you wake up in is a winter room.
The man you love has come in a dream
to wave goodbye from a 1950 Buick.
You push the cat off the bed
and slide your feet to the floor.
Placing a cup of coffee on the end of the ironing board,
you spread a blouse,
making it ready for the reassuring steam.
Every day you will do something for the last time.

To a Man in Kansas

I'm doing the dishes in Winooski, Vermont
and thinking of you.
These are not your children in the next room.
These are not your dishes.
From Wichita my sister writes
to say she planted larkspur on your grave.
I watch a crow standing still beside the road.
Before I finish the dishes the crow is gone.
It is going to rain tomorrow.
I marry you again.

Coming Back, I Visit Myself

I knock twice on the door
of the old apartment.
A woman lets me in.
My silver toiletries. My plants.
My knife and fork and napkin.
I look to see what has died or been given away
but everything is here.

I say nothing.
I am not supposed to say anything.
I poke my head in the closet
looking for the good green dress.

Watching

I watch a hawk turn,
dropping the sun off its wings.

My mother stared at the darkness
that sat on her hands.
At the end
she tried to shake it loose.

Next Door

Next door the old man and the old woman come out
as they do every day
for a walk to the corner and back.
They pause at the edge of the porch.
Down one step, he turns to the woman
and waits.
I think she is trying to remember
where they are going.

I wish I were first
in your life again.

For T.

You have been dead four days
and nothing comforts me except
that crow on the lawn, foraging.

The Paper Xylophone

You witness your madness.
First you build the xylophone from paper
in your office.
Then the feathered nose-piece.
You send for a parakeet.
You begin not to answer your phone.
After knocking, friends go away.
Needing the right sound,
you snap the parakeet
like a bean.

The Tractor Driver's Funeral

I go because he worked on my father's farm.
The pallbearers' coats are too loose or too tight.
What the widow wears is
pink and wrong.
At the cemetery I touch her
but she doesn't remember.

I lie on my bed and drop my shoes to the floor.
In the bathroom my husband brushes his teeth.
I put on the black gown.

A Woman Married to Grief

When they met, the woman didn't think
it would last.
She said to herself she would tire of him after awhile.

She knows now that she will never leave.
She has become proud to be seen with him.
Whenever they go out,
she puts on a hat with a wide brim.

Remembering a Sunny Climate

The old woman folds clothes
and puts them away
while the old man naps on the couch.
They have said nothing to each other all day,
but in the woman's mind they talk as they did
and work in the vineyards
and stir in each other's arms at night
while the pear trees drop their blooms.

Emerson County Shaping Dream

Any girl in Emerson County
knows what dreams are for—
Daddy in the shape of a rich boy.
She chooses him who chooses her,
dreamed in the shape of his mama.
Their house is happy
if the girl is pretty, if he likes the things
she says to him,
if the boy has land from his daddy—flat, not hilly,
if she loves the way he loves on her.
The bank holds all their papers
but nobody mentions this.
One day
a man from a neighboring county
smiles at the girl.
They begin to meet
at the Albert Pick, or the Claridge.
Nobody mentions this either.

Audiences

Audiences are so lonely
as the curtain falls
on the groom and bride or
the opera star or the corpse.
The lights go up and those in the audience
raise their eyes.
They talk softer or louder,
knowing they address a dark
into which those important ones are gone.
They head for home, for coffee, for a phone.
It doesn't matter.

Becoming Invisible

a found poem, from the archives of Arkansas folklore

It is possible to become invisible.
Follow a few simple steps.
First, you catch a toad.
Put it in a clay planter,
the type with a hole in the bottom.
The first full moon
take it out to the graveyard.
Find a grave with an ant hill on it.
Put the toad on the ant hill;
cover it with the pot.
The next full moon
go back and get the toad's bones.
Take them home and stand in front of a mirror.
Place the bones
one at a time in your mouth
until you find the one that makes you invisible.

There are 192 bones in a toad.

The House Facing Dahlia

In the house next door facing Dahlia,
Ardeliah Soames—whose front yard flourished
with sunflower whirligigs,
cement flamingos, and a cat she called Malone—
died today.

Saturdays there had come a black boy mowing the lawn,
each Saturday for three years or so.
She called the boy Floyd. His name was Foster.

Today, in a tie and suit
Foster came after they took Mrs. Soames away.
He weeded both sides of the walk.

Foster took a sunflower as he left
and one of the pink flamingos,
still inclined and delicate
under his arm.

The Day After the Bottomlands Farmer Lost His Wife

he brought a hired woman to the house
to cook his meals.
People talked. She was not the customary black,
but a white woman off the river
who smoked, who wore, winter and summer,
Red Ball boots.
She and the farmer almost never spoke.
After supper
she cleared the table
and set it for breakfast.
She put cornbread on a plate
beneath a napkin
and turned his water glass
mouth down.

Stopping My Car for the Light

Stopping my car for the light,
I smile as a man and a dog cross the street.
I smile because they don't know who I am
or that you are gone;
also because
the man is apparently not thinking anything
and the dog stops to yawn.

Between the Wars

No one else is in the diner
except a man and a woman
dancing with their eyes closed.
The juke box is playing "For All We Know."

After Seeing a Movie about the American Bombing of Cambodia

Undressing for bed, I think about Cambodia's grief.
That isn't true;
I think about you, gone,
and no way to find you.

You may be eating now, or reading a paper
in a room I'll never see.
The wisteria we planted
has twisted its way to the roof.

After the Quarrel

My car follows yours
down the mountain road
scattering crows and gravel.
At the highway we turn
our backs to one another.

A Farm Wife Laments Her Husband's Absence

At sunset the house cools, popping.
The snow that began last night
went on all day.
Snow climbs the windows.
It covers everything:
the hedge behind the house, the barn,
the poplar tree taller than the barn.
When the snow stops
I inch the 4x4 into town
knowing you're not there.
But a man getting out of his car
pushes his hair back
the way you do.

The Other Side

My mother dresses chickens.
My father reads.
I call to them.
They glance up, annoyed.

Hearing Tractors

After the bank takes the farm,
the farmer's wife goes back, invisible,
to live there again.
She watches the owners
take down the kitchen curtains.
She watches them plant cornflowers along the walk.
In town, her body believes
it waxes the old furniture,
hears tractors
in the traffic far below her window.

When the Buck or Two Steakhouse Changed Hands

They put plastic over the menus.
They told the waitresses to wear white shoes.
They fired Rita.
They threw out the unclaimed keys
and the pelican with a toothpick
that bowed as you left.

1942

My father's harmonica came off the mantel every night.
He played it while my mother sang
until they went to bed.
The last songs were always
"Working on the Railroad," "O Susanna,"
and "Sam," a song my mother invented.
Whenever the paper said
someone in our town was killed
or missing in action,
my father wouldn't take the harmonica down
even if
it was no one we knew.

A Girl in a Sundress

enters a café.
A woman drinking beer in a booth
remembers one August, one Sunday.

A fresh dress
stiff with starch.
All afternoon she waits for him by the lake.
That night lying under the fan
she promises not to let it
happen again.

The girl in the sundress
looks at the woman
but not as if there is anything between them.

Dancing Man

The music in Mick's Bar tonight
is three parts smoke and one part hard down blues.
The man who brought me is drinking bourbon shots and beer.
The woman in the next booth shouts
Play something for me Play something slow for me.

I turn for another drink
and one of the men on the dance floor
has on your brown hat,
three guinea feathers in the hat band.
But you are in Mexico, or Greece.

I would leave with him,
let him do whatever he wanted to do
if he would keep the hat on.

The Privileged

They homestead
a square of harsh country
in the Maine of their imagination.

Almost every week
they dig potatoes in sleet.
Three hundred miles from the nearest doctor,
the baby dies in fever;
the horse dies too.

They will never give it up,
that place where he gives her bruises big as pears,
where she scratches
blood-pearls and blooms on his face.

How else can they endure,
two privileged people
in a town just west of Topeka,
the wheat fields, the houses with wide porches
lying all about them?

Progress

I stand beside my mother's winter grave.

I consider that when I have slipped into that darkness
and then been followed there by my children and theirs
she will not cross anybody's mind.

I touch the earth exactly, I think, above her heart.

The Gift

Fireflies send their codes from the grass
like signals from a difficult coast.

I want to thank you
for climbing the steep road to my cabin,
for bringing wine,
for humming off-key in the dark.

Here is a book with all the letters of our names.

Towns Facing Railroads

1991

A Friendly Town

The chamber of commerce was glad to give me a map.
I saw a creek curving its southern border,
the Burlington Northern dividing east from west,
streets named Elm and Locust and Park
stringing it together.
Tonight, after moving in,
I walk to a place where one of those streets deadends.
I say to myself that being a stranger is not
knowing what lies behind these wide windows.

Burying My Mother

In the rooms of my mother's brain
by one, by two, the jiggers of light went out.
She climbed her apartment steps
a year at a time.

As I walk from her grave to my car
Napoleon's horses cut through snow
crossing Russia, Hannibal's armies
take the Alps, Stonehenge
is laid.

A Veteran of the War Speaks of the Enemy

He glistens in our dreams.
We have no other enemies before him.
Our sons and daughters will have to make do
with lesser ones.
Ours, treacherous, foul, teeth rotting,
is what we want. We seek him daily,
listening for his cough, his swaggered breathing.
We devour him in thanksgiving.
Living long into our pensions,
we will lick him clean.

Snow Comes to Pittsburg, Kansas

The men in Harry's Café predict snow.
Seen in Fort Scott, they say, headed here.

Behind Willie Nelson a harmonica whines.
I think of a man I knew.

At the counter a woman taps her fingernails
against the formica.
At the sound the men fall silent.

Edge of America

In Kansas City, I'm shopping
the Sharper Image.
They've got the ocean on tape.
I step back ten years
to Maine, Mt. Desert Island, Thunder Hole
where, if you stand too close,
the ocean rages through a needle
and pulls thunder through your spine.
We hold each other, deaf and terrified.
Alone, safe and not far
from the exact center of the United States,
I think of the edge of America,
the gulls screaming around us like burning cats.

Small Town at Dusk

Cars on the bypass
move between places with restaurants
we have forgotten the names of.
Fireflies appear and disappear.
Night takes the sidewalks first
and then the marigolds and the sprinklers,
the children's skates.
Nothing argues with the ambling dogs
except the tree frogs and the occasional slamming
of a screen door.

A Stand of Pines

I knew I'd never stay on my father's farm,
hating the clay fields,
the corner stand of pines,
helping my father skin rabbits,
jacket and pants.
I left one night when the moon set.

Today as I pass a field, the patient figures of two mules,
memory stitches my skin
clean as the treadle Singer
clacking after supper into darkness,
clacking all night and into the rising chores.

Farm Wife

In this drought
pole beans will cycle early.
One day as she is driving to town alone,
the car dies on the highway.
The sounds of passing cars
are like the sounds children make
of the sounds of cars.
Her husband withers like the wheat.
He's been in town since yesterday,
drinking down the smell of dead cows.

How We Live

Walking out of Food 4 Less,
we see a car thrash over the curb,
heading for us like a speedboat.
The driver's face
is like the face of someone
stepping back from a table saw,
seeing that he has cut off his thumb.

In the Coffee Shops

of towns facing railroads
where the grocery and the P.O.
look across a highway at rails the trains forgot,
chatter clicks into silence
when somebody new walks in.
Then the folk of Jerome or Black Coffee or Start,
in Mama Dan's or Della's or The Mallard
light another cigarette.
Dishes continue to break
dreamily in the kitchen.

The Dress

Well, I'm her mother, and I cannot see it,
that kind of money for one more thing to wear
to the Frostee-Freeze. I guess I might have done
the same thing at her age but, hell, at her age
I was married and lived at the mining camp
raising two kids, the baby being her.
She put on the dress last night, a strapless thing,
slipping up from the bottom and down at the top.
She called Harold, the weenie boyfriend,
to come take her down to the Idle Hour.
Waiting, she crossed her legs and fluffed her hair.
I'll bet she wasn't dreaming of pukey babies
or a man who rolls away soon as he's done,
or even of herself, married willy-nilly,
tomtit for a husband and no money.
It cost what she makes in a week, but she's got to have it.

Farewell, Dusky Seaside

a found poem, from Time, *June 29, 1987*

Six inches from tip to tail,
the tiny brown birds made
their home in a ten-mile coastal stretch of marsh
near Titusville, Florida.
When development from nearby Cape Canaveral
began to encroach,
they stubbornly refused to move,
and their number declined
relentlessly.
Last week
the last known Dusky Seaside Sparrow
expired: Orange Band, a twelve-year-old male,
was found dead in his cage.

Scientists tried
to save the bird from extinction by crossbreeding it
with a hardier sparrow. But Orange Band died
before they could complete the job,
leaving five hybrid Dusky Seasides—one of them
seven-eighths pure.

Item, Page Three

I am waiting for the news that fits to find me:
    Woman Loses Arm to Brown Recluse
    Mother of Two Assaulted
    Resident Missing at Sea
    Poet Dies More or Less Old
never having written what she could hear
humming like crickets,
ancient and daily,
scattering before her feet.

The Visiting Assistant Professor on the First Day Addresses Another Class in Yet Another Town

She looks at the red-haired boy
in the third row.
She remembers a Cajun boy
in the last town
who sat on the low branch of a live-oak
the day she held class under the trees,
the day she read
"I Saw in Louisiana a Live-Oak Growing,"
who dropped down from the branch after the poem
and dropped the class.

I'll Be Seeing You

World War II is slipping away, I can feel it.
Its officers are gray.
Their wives who danced at the USO
are gray, too.
Veterans forget their stories. Some lands they fought in
have new names, and Linda Venetti
who deserted the husband who raised cows
to run off with an officer
has come home to look after her mother
and work the McDonald's morning shift.
William Holden is dead,
and my mother, who knew all the words
to "When the Lights Go On Again All Over the World."

At the Marriott

I dream of an old hotel,
tile floors cool in summer,
windows velvet-draped against the heat
as I wait for the phone beside the bed to ring
and him to cross town.
The phone rings. A voice belonging to no one tells me
it is six a.m.

On Catalpa Street

At dusk, when kitchen-window light
settles on the grass like a picnic cloth,
he thinks of the town he lived in
when he was twelve,
the year his father died.
He remembers an evening after his father's funeral,
crossing the yards wide with dogs and mowers
toward the yellow light of the living room,
toward a baseball game on the radio,
a back porch that smelled like sour mops.
He remembers a man he had never seen before
sitting with his mother at the kitchen table,
his mother looking, turning toward him
as though he might have been the Perkins boy
come to paint the shed.

Buying a House

The people who live here have left
to let me look.
The real estate lady struggles with the key.
I see the half bath, the den, the dining nook,
black shoes with cracks across the toes,
seed catalogs and toothpaste.
I should not be in this house.
There is something here I'm supposed to understand.

Homeplace

Awake while you sleep,
I tie and untie the strings of what went wrong:
the farm auctioned, my father buried in Minnesota,
you and I alone
in a rented room.

I remember my father when I was six
pushing open a gate on the farm road,
stirring the dust of August.
The locusts sizzling in the grass,
a hum of dragonflies hanging sleepy above us.

Driving Kansas

Skimming over macadam, Topeka to Hays,
I see a goat on the roof of a house
under a sky-blue sky.
Goat, hats off to you, I say
and raise my fist out the window.
The cold bites me like God.

Coyotes trot beside the highway.
I'm climbing into a land of limestone,
scattered tufts of grass,
no trees.
It is mid-afternoon.
I think of the
occasional house tonight
blinking itself awake as it drowns in the unending wheat.

Rooms

Whenever I see someone loading a car
with a Walkman, baskets, a rolled rug,
I think of what is left in the rooms
where people I have never met
argue or eat or pull on their socks.
Blindfolded, I could walk you through those rooms.
I could find, if I needed to, a needle I used once,
fallen between the boards.

Working Late in My Studio on the Second Story

Sounds from the bypass drift up.
On the ground floor, a clock and the kitchen tick.
A cat yawns, pulling sleep out of the carpet.
My dead mother, who must be white as maggots now,
slips her voice under the front door.
I nod myself awake,
hoping I've been asleep.

Neighborhood

There is rage in the woman's voice
coming from a house close by.
Perhaps he is drunk again or home
smelling of women.
Her voice
shakes the catalpas.
The moon climbs over the town,
erasing windows.

Dead Child

It lived a week.
In the house, such fury.
The child's cries, chairs scraping, things boiling on the stove.
And always the child, its voice at chimney tops.

Then silences and whimpers.
The doctor's face.
The church,
the whisper of the coffin being wheeled out
like the rustle a last student makes
leaving the room on the last day of a semester.

Most of the Time

My mother sifts in my memory.
I can choose to see her
or not.
But last night as I tried to sleep,
she leaned across the bed and stared at me
and called me
somebody else's name.

A Bottomlands Farmer Suffers a Sea Change

A man fits a key into the door of an office in Chicago.
Suddenly he remembers a plowed field.
He remembers the farm
before they took it.
He remembers walking its ditches,
flushing birds.

In a park across the street
pigeons scatter.
He hurries into the office
where a phone is ringing.

Fields

Driving the interstate from Little Rock to Conway,
I see rice growing in the fields.
It is green as crème de menthe.
The levees are dark chocolate.
I want to stuff the fields into my mouth.

Four P.M.

Now come A. J. Spence and wife
before bankruptcy court to pray
forgiveness of creditors, to say
how the hole in their lives grew
to take her mother's jewelry,
the ninety acres, and the cows.
Now come counsel and trustee;
now A. J. Spence and spouse
swear before God and furled flag
that then and now and here and there
they do relinquish and forsake
for any who come and any who care.

Marbles

I talk to my class about place.
Consider, I say, Tilbury Town, Gardiner, the Saginaw.
Some look at their hands
as if they are holding the words there
like marbles.

You appear in the door
from the Prairie Grove of our school days.
We go off to the playground and trade cats-eyes.

When I get back to the classroom
no one has noticed except maybe one student
who looks as though he lost the thread of my talk
or a pencil.

His Funeral

She despises the way funerals lie,
despises the baby's breath and wax leaves,
the undertakers
standing with their hands behind their backs.

She takes a seat directly behind the widow.
She remembers his body,
the motel rooms
and the way he fretted about hiding the cars.

The preacher is saying something about the children.
She wonders what the wife knew,
what happens to the body first
and how soon.

Surviving in Kansas

for Richard Blum

A man told me this
at a party in Topeka.
Bugs in Kansas, he said,
sleep on the roots of grasses.
There are no trees in Kansas.
Bugs go underground.
If you pull up the grasses
you'll find them.

Nearly certain this was a lie,
I asked him to dance with me.

Story

Decades ago
in a small, mad town,
there is an evangelist, soon to be my father,
with black, brilliantined hair.
Standing before the borrowed pulpit, shoes buried in sawdust,
he marries my mother with his eyes.
He leaves her before I am born,
taking his Bible with him
and her mother's brooch.

My daughters love the story.
At five and seven they are already turned
toward someplace else,
they and others like them raised in towns
of summer revivals, visiting preachers,
the one wide highway out.

Talking with You Long Distance

I get what I want.
You say it: It's your fault.

The wallpaper roses blur and fade.
A silver bowl on the table
has taken a skin of dust.

Packing

I want to come home.
I have been too many years in the rooms of others.
I am looking for
tall windows,
fireflies on the lawn.
Packing the last box again,
I watch the dark condense
across the grass.

The Day

You realize you'll remember it
as you leaf through a magazine
try on a hat
miss a plane.

He says he's leaving. You'll remember the way
he takes his shirts out of the drawer,
refolds each one.
The way your stomach turns
quick as you'd shake a spider
off a sleeve.

Children's Children

They watch from the silver ovals
I have caught them in,
boys and girls about to enter
the other side of time
although I speak to them often on the phone
and they send letters telling me
how, gently, with sweet apologies,
each in appointed turn begins to live
in days I'll see
on the backs of photographs.

Once in Winter

when snow fell light as ashes,
we walked Times Square.
Turning to kiss you,
I saw a man lie down in a doorway,
fitting himself
to the stone.

The Stump

When they lost the farm near Omaha
and their money,
the farmer's wife thought of it
as losing an arm.
The stump was a challenge.
It was, she said,
for the time being.
A healthy arm would sprout
if she were patient and wise and a hard worker.
But the stump healed smooth.
She watched things disappear:
the TV, the car, her teeth,
and still the stump offered nothing.
One night she began to understand
it would be with her always,
mean as a pig.

In the Home of the Famous Dead

The perfect visit. We pay and we go in,
the way we first enter a hospital room
except that we don't have to talk to anyone
and the men if they wear hats keep them on.
We know this is not the house they knew,
not the way they knew it, anyway,
when they were eating and laughing and having colds.
The best furniture has been removed, and the rugs.
What's left, the chintz and brass, is pissy stuff.
Still, there's a whiff of bacon in the kitchen.
We shuffle along beside the velvet ropes,
subdued. A small boy tries to cross under,
not yet afraid of dustless, perfect rooms.

Her Last Trick

Sit down and loosen your collar.
Let me take your coat.
Isn't this a nice hotel? We'll order wine.
I'm glad you like my dress. I always pretend
I'm invited to dinner with some rich old man
when I buy my clothes.
Well, here's to us.
You're married, right? Me, too. I got three children.
Hey, this is a business, like anything else.
That isn't what I meant.
There's something I want to tell you
before we start. This is on me.
You're surprised? Surprise is what we live for. Why else
would you be here?

The First Warm Day

Watching you take hammer and nails to your roof
is like seeing the shadow of my mother move
behind the screen door of a farmhouse on an Ohio hill
in April when trees stutter and tulips find
their old pattern and a clear creek moves
behind the gym of the high school where boys remember
spring and turn to their cars and highways
in search of girls on porches
protected by leaves that turn an even deeper green
because I am watching you take hammer and nails to your roof.

Remodeling

My mother fell flat on her porch the day it iced over
while she was gone to the store for a quart of milk.
I think it would be like that if she came back now
to hear us hammering on her house, whistling.

Growing Up on the Bayou de Glaises

Light would climb the walls of the sitting room,
wavering when a wind shook the water,
slipping in ribbons
across the only two pictures in the house:
Huey P. and Jesus.

Salesman

He sits in Bob's Grill,
the large gray leather case between his feet.
Unfolding the morning paper
he reads about a woman's body
found by the bypass,
her eyes, the sheriff says,
eaten by birds.

Humanities 113

A shoe, then a bucket at the beach, then a pet
slides through a dark slot
with no explanation from anybody.
Then a grandmother, then a friend.
I read from Thomas Hardy.
We are talking about
Literature and Death.
A girl on the front row yawns,
stretching a slender arm
toward the tall boy beside her.

A Woman of Substance

Every day
his dead wife argues with him.
She argues and rocks and argues,
shelling peas.

Catalpa

for Ann and Steve Meats

When I am old and no longer able to remember
Shakespeare's Sonnet 73
or the names of my children
I hope I can call up when I want to
one catalpa bloom
balanced on the toe of my shoe.

Blessing

My neighbor hangs out the morning wash
and a storm dances up.
She strips the line,
the children's pajamas with the purple ducks,
her husband's shorts,
the panties she has hidden under a sheet.
When the sun comes out
she comes back
with the panties and the sheets, the shorts and the pajamas.
This is my ritual, not hers.
May her husband never stop drinking and buy her a dryer.

Upon Hearing about the Suicide of the Daughter of Friends

Something called to her that Sunday afternoon, perhaps,
that she could not name.
You and I cannot name it, drawn to each other
by this news.
The young cry when they feel it
breathing beside them.
We may know it sometimes through its disguises,
say the sound of a car at two a.m.
grinding to a stop in a gravel drive.

To Her

I get up
from the cold bed,
open the door.
Someone with his hand at my back
pushes me into a room with a bed
where I am sleeping.
The woman in the bed will not wake up
although I beat on her chest
a long time.

Night Flight, Delta #481

We are rising up from Boston
heading for Bangor, Maine.
The flight attendant's smile
hangs before us.
A tube and a mask make circles in the air.

Once, in New Orleans, on Decatur Street
you drew yourself into a ring of chalk.
You danced to the skittering music from Mollie's Bar,
clicking the change in your pockets like castanets.
You stepped over the circle and disappeared
into the crowd.
I have looked for you—
by rivers,
in depots, on loading docks.
A man on skates,
a man bending to pet his cat,
a man running across a darkening street
is finally you.
He is not.

I turn out my reading light.
Pretending to touch your arm
I touch the window beside me,
cold as it passes through the stars.

They Agree to Call It Off but Then

She fixes a drink and forgets where it is.
She thinks how soon
others will bring her drinks of water
and smooth a blanket over her knees.
She hears the neighbor's children after school,
the thinning traffic.
She leaves a message on his machine:
Meet me in Wichita.
Wear the yellow shirt.
Answer your phone.

Dropping a Line

Six months have passed
and no word.
I am playing hopscotch on the page.
I skip everything I need to tell you.
If I cross a line or step on a stone
I am lost. I will not get into Heaven.
Therefore, I do not say Come back,
it is dark.

I send you this letter
without a line you can use.

From Darkening Porches

1996

What Happens When We Leave

Leaving a room, we remember arriving,
the first turning of the key,
the room, pristine and startled,
opening to take us in.
Dropping the key on the bureau,
we open a door
someplace else.

Behind us now, the room goes mute.
The morning paper sifts to the floor,
ticking itself to sleep.
The desk and chair and table,
nothing expected of them,
settle their hands behind them
like morticians at the church.

The sound of a crow.
Then the electric sweeper. The witch inside it
boiling the carpet.

Late afternoon.
A simmer of traffic. A far train.

Then dusk.
Silence deepens in the room,
seamless as an apple
or a fox.

Then footsteps.
Outside the door the brushing of a sleeve,
someone else with the expectant key,
absently humming.

Nights and Days

Nights, the dream.
I'm on a dirt road
trying to outrun Kansas:
blisters in the farmhouse paint,
ripples in the wheat
like horsehide under flies.
Days, wind rounding the corners of the house
like a warp of bees.

She Reflects upon a Sadness

She will not say
that it was ennobling, that there must have been
a purpose.

She will say
that if it had not happened
she might not feel this rush of joy
like a blush
at the sight of a hawk dropping into a ditch,
ignoring the traffic, taking
what it needs.

Circus

The elephants entered town
from some country the other side of God.
As solemn and as bored as saints,
they seemed to step to music
we couldn't hear.
Then men with tents and costumes
and ropes as big as trees
swarmed the lot across from the drive-in.

When the young trapezist
swam the air to his death
that hazy afternoon,
I didn't see it.
I was watching the elephants turn in the ring
like toys winding down.
I was watching dust
turn in the light like sequins.

Then, always on a night we weren't thinking of it,
the circus would leave.
I was glad to see it go
although it has taken me
nearly a lifetime
to admit it.

A Bottomlands Farmer Deals with the Arkansas Power and Light Transmission Towers Set in His Field

for Jim Spicer

He resents what they take:
his best field, the one that drained right,
a road his grandfather built.
Since they set the towers
his cows don't calve.
The bald spot in the winter wheat
could hold six tractors abreast.
Maybe he'll sell the place.
But who'd want it now?

The farmer sees his father under a full moon,
riding the bucking Farmall, plowing straight.
"Always somebody out there," he used to say,
"biding his time."

Radio

The house on Mickle Road.
Ten o'clock evenings,
my father turning off his Philco,
the orange light reluctant to go.
And didn't the brocade where the sound came out
get hot, and smell?
I think it did, a faint scorching,
the brocade a shade of brown
you don't find anymore.

Eight Years a Ghost

He thinks I keep his things.
He thinks I hear him whistling.
He thinks he's making a racket
on the stairs.

The Time of Their Lives

At the cinema
they find their lives.
The years stop nattering.
There's music
as they take off their clothes, or kiss.
Their bodies glimmer
like dolphins in moonlight.
The lights go up:
The black floor. The dirty popcorn.
The man and the woman
suddenly pale and blinking.

The Crib at Buffalo Antiques

I touch the crib,
seeing the mother and the father and the preacher,
the wind on a hill,
the shovels nicking the small stones.

Spinsters

In that house
a radio was keeping its dull distance.
A clock struck in the metallic way a rooster announces day.
One of the women sat in a bedroom,
sewing on a treadle machine
in fits and starts
as if listening for something:
a burglar perhaps, or the dog recruiting a shoe
for the porch.
Neither happened.
A breeze stirred up dust from the stockyards next door
and a cousin called
from Minneapolis.

The Duplex

It's a little run down, but okay. I hope
we can afford it, with layoffs at the plant,
one baby sick, another on the way.
The neighborhood is iffy, but it sure beats the trailer.

Dwayne, my husband, put up the swing set
over there next to that little maple.
I wish this place had another tree.
The babies, they'll come to use it later, of course;
for now, the swing set is for Jimmy. He's five
this October, going to pre-school.
We got it cheap. It looks real good though,
all red and green and shining, the slide so polished
the clouds look like they're bouncing right in your face.

Dwayne and me had an argument about it.
He said it cost too much. I said I'd scrimp.
Sometimes it's hard to be a proper wife.
I don't like going against Dwayne

but you've got to give your kids advantages.
I never saw a swing till I started school.
Dwayne had it worse. Maybe that's what's wrong.

The rooms next door are rented, but we don't know who
or whether they'll have kids the right age.
Or whether we'll want them to. I'm nervous about it.
What if they smell? What if they talk funny?
There'll be hell to pay with Dwayne, I'll tell you.

And what if they're the kind to disappear,
to move away in the night, loading the car

with what all they can take, stealing something,
maybe taking the whole swing set?

What would I ever say to Jimmy?
Dwayne would cuss me first, then call the police.

I'm glad we have the set. I truly am.
This way, Jimmy can pick and choose his friends.

I know what Dwayne will do if who moves in
isn't right. Whoever it is, I tell you,
better not be single, pregnant and five kids,

and using food stamps. Or plop herself
and her cigarettes down every morning in my kitchen.
Or mess with that little tree.
I just hope they're clean.

A Southerner in Kansas Recalls Trees

Living without them, she takes solace
in hedges or in weeds.
Some nights,
alone in the house,
she lies face down on the wood floor.

Just Off the Highway

It is an ugly spread.
Everything leans, even the house.
The grounds are bare, the butane tank and the shed
aloof in dirt.
Afternoons, a train sends sounds
that ripple under the grass.
Someone in the house opens a window partway and plays,
on what is still a piano,
"You Are My Lucky Star."

A Farmer Dies

He leaves ninety acres and a house.
In the kitchen,
a bowl of dusty pears.
In the orchard, leaves are turning to rust
as if it might not ever
rain again.
Someone will have to stay and sell the cows.

Fear

A man and wife
sit at a delicatessen.
A young woman strolls in.
With her come sun and rain
and stars over a clear lake.
The man looks at the girl
in a way his wife has almost forgotten.

Air Midwest Lands on Ice at Kansas City International

We taxi onto the apron
fast and slow and fast
as if the plane is looking for a dock.
Slowly I remember another evening.
Summer fishing with my grandfather,
caught by the dark, stragglers
looking for the right house and pier.
My grandfather finds the slot
and slips us in,
the outboard sputtering to silence
and smelling like a match just struck.
A light from my grandmother's kitchen
dozes on the water.

Needing Noise

After the child died,
the mother and the father ran the accident
continually in their minds.
It repeated itself like an old teacher.
Sooner or later
the remaining children fell
from their parents' lives.

Days moved like stones.
The cocktail hour. The evening meal.

They watched television,
night after night,
disappointed.

She Feels Out of Place in Burl's Auto Service

She gets out of her car.
A man, holding his Automotive Ready-Light,
slides under a lifted truck.
A man in coveralls strolls toward her.
On the radio, a country singer decides
about women and men.

The Young Dressmaker, Best in Emerson County

Everybody who knew anything about dressmaking
said it was a shame
a person didn't wear the garments Vera Hefley made
so you could see the wrong side.
They admired
the vanishing points of the darts,
the graceful easing of the set-in sleeves.

I thought
she should have been dancing.
A man should have had his hand
at the small of her back.
They should have been in a tango
back and forth
throughout that miserable house.

A Bottomlands Farmer's Widow Remarries and Speaks of the Killing

There's not much to tell different from anybody's
tale of woe. One summer we owned the Lincoln,
next we didn't. Too much sun, then it rained all March.
Mother blamed the Lincoln on Darrell—that was my husband.
She said he was drinking. Would you like a scotch?

After the Lincoln went, things got bad.
More rotted crops, then Darrell and the trial,
then Mother died. Times when night comes down
smelling like a cottonmouth, I can see her
there at the trial, that satisfied look she got
when the lawyers held up the panty hose and bra
Darrell was supposed to be wearing the night he was killed.
A certain waitress named Nelda testified
he'd got drunk that night hustling three boys.

I got married again last Christmas. The farm was auctioned
right off the courthouse steps. My new husband, Jared,
he takes old Lincolns and fixes them up like new.
Those boys, they got thirty years apiece.

I barely think about it anymore.
A scale of one to ten, I'd put it six,
what with the farm and the baby and my oldest, Ginny,
which I don't know to this day
where she is.

Dreaming the Kin

Climbing that dark hill again,
I see my grandfather in a field of corn.
I wave to him. He doesn't see me.
I move on to the barn
where dust motes hang like stars
in an unsteady heaven.

I enter my grandmother's kitchen.
Canning sausage, she doesn't look up.
My aunt sits folding clothes, her back to me.
Laughing, they speak of people I've never known.
Perhaps I've come to the wrong house,
though the table is set with the dishes I remember—
white, with red and yellow flowers chipping on the rims.

After Vietnam/Standing at a Window at Gate 2

A flight comes in.
The coffin, out of Baggage,
glistens like an ocarina.
So lightly she might be caressing a burn,
a woman touches the window.

Many Mansions

Ernestine came Thursdays
to do my mother's wash.
She was black and smelled of starch,
her voice polite as the breeze
that tapped the kitchen curtains.
The child she brought with her one summer
sat on the back stoop and never spoke.

His eyes, storm-dull and solemn,
come to mind as I think of my mother in her last days
when she seemed to see something so desolate
she could not turn away.

I guessed the boy to be four or five.
Ernestine didn't know.
He was her sister's boy,
sent down from Chicago.

After a Neighbor's House Was Broken Into

She said it was like falling asleep in a rented room
and the landlord comes,
singing an aria from *Aida*,
snapping open the blinds like you'd snap green beans
and helping himself to chocolates on the table.

Admission

On the outskirts of a carnival near Pueblo
a fox and a shrike amble by.
In a quarter-turn the fox becomes a man,
the shrike a woman.
He smiles through his rusty mustache.
Her polished nails curl inward
as she links her arm in his,
resting a hand on his sleeve.
They enter
the mad and sizzling lights.

Driving a Louisiana Highway, Past a Town with a Ruined Depot, She Remembers the Negro Albino in Her Hometown

His lips were too thick for the whites
and the blacks didn't like his freckles
and red hair.
Each summer Saturday,
sitting on my parents' porch,
I'd see the albino cutting the Brylie sisters' yard,
pushing the mower lazily back and forth
while one or the other sister watched.
Thinking they knew just what caused some albinos,
everybody in town named the white father,
a former mayor who'd died of cancer
and left his farm to the church.
The mowing finished,
the albino would wait on the back steps
until one of the sisters, fanning herself,
opened the screen door a notch
and handed him a dollar.

For years I haven't thought of the albino.
Now, driving past this town,
I see the years and towns. I see the one
I'll probably die a stranger in,
like him.

A Picture

In this picture
my mother younger than I am now
is in the kitchen,
singeing pin feathers over the gas range.
My brother is five and has not yet fallen
beneath the tractor.

In Ray's Café

A girl in a far booth
is breast-feeding a baby.
The man sitting across the table from me
stirs his coffee.
Where were you last night till four a.m., I say.
Someone starts the jukebox.
The girl shifts the baby to her shoulder
while she talks on the phone.
The baby wails.
The man sitting across from me signals the waitress,
careful not to break the noise between us.

What Part of Town Was That In?

A boy and a girl sit on a park bench.
Stick figures.
As I walk toward them, they draw themselves
fingernails and noses.
    The gun as dull as stovepipe.
    They will take my earrings
    and my watch.
Passing them, I glance behind me.
I see them on the park bench,
erasing their fingernails and noses,
stick figures again.
I walk on,
past brightening houses.

My Mother's Dead Dresses

They wake me from sleep.
Peach, magenta, red,
her young dresses
my father loved to touch.
They are 1940s dresses,
some with tiny zippers at the waist.
I wonder where in that lost house
my father has put them.

Vast

She took a snapshot of Kansas in June.
Endless sky blue as L.A. swimming pools,
endless grass green as Kentucky.
She framed it, hung it on the wall.
Turning from the room,
she didn't hear the avalanche,
sky and grass
spilling endlessly out of the frame.

Someone will find her
in due time.

How It Sometimes Happens to a Man That a Noble Heart and Purpose Come to Dwell within Him

A man goes home to his wife,
thinking of a woman he has been with
that afternoon.
Kissing his wife and taking off his coat,
    he remembers how the woman
    unbuttoned her blouse.
After supper he sits with his drink on the darkening porch.
He would like to give to the woman
his love, his life, his father's
pocket watch.
He hears his wife
knitting in the dark.

Singer at the Farmers' Market

Walking onto the makeshift stage
she thinks how she can never
lay down all she knows,
the suicides of friends, two marriages failed,
a daughter gone morose and wrong.

Tonight, in this open arena, a breeze lifts her hair.
Her voice frays a little in the damp air
to bring the people back to the old loves,
a house, a street, a town.

Depot

Unchanged in thirty years,
they sometimes step onstage
beside that depot
where my husband and I first saw them
in a Georgia town we were driving through at dawn:
a father and son, or so I've imagined them,
the son in Army uniform extending his hand to the man
who hesitates and turns away.
I saw a father's rejection of a son.
My husband saw an ongoing struggle
against despicable tears.
Thus they came to live inside our lives,
keeping their ordinary secrets to themselves.

A Story to Tell

Red's Tree Service was printed in an arc
across the dented pickup door.
She noted the men's tattoos.
She looked down at her blouse,
checking the buttons.

She pointed to the pin-oak a storm had uprooted.
The men walked around it. They argued.
They quoted a price.
It seemed to be within reason.

Still, standing there with them in the drive,
she told them Thanks but no.
Then she saw the girl, eighteen maybe,
sitting inside the truck, half smiling,
as if this is what you ought to expect
in a place where everybody has three-car garages
and ferns on their porch. Hadn't
she said?

Pulling the rusty pickup back into the street,
the driver grated through the gears.

The woman hesitated in front of the house.
Maybe she'd paint the trim a yellow.
Or a blue.

Later she invited the couple next door for drinks
on the glassed-in porch.
From somewhere down the street, the sounds of children.

A wasp in the room
shuffled its wings like paper.

She told them the story: The men. The tree.
She didn't mention
the girl.
The couple gave her a name to call—
somebody who would do a good job,
somebody who had been around for years.

She Ponders the Doctor's Diagnosis

The wind before a storm
flushes a paper sack out of a ditch.
The grasses in the ditch quiver.
She thinks of her mother so recently under ground,
in a frenzy of being changed.

Everything You Wanted

It sits beside a hill north of a town
named Miner's Grove or Franklin,
a farmhouse like any other in Kansas:
two-storied, white, bleak under four trees.
Behind it a windmill, a barn, a shed.
In the barn, the flaring smell of dung.
Room by room
sunlight blooms in the house,
polishes each table like a wife.
Here is everything
you wanted.

Someone enters stage left,
a husband maybe, or the eldest son
to hang himself in the cloudy breath of the milking shed.

Address

A policeman, sent to tell the husband,
goes by moonlight to the address in the woman's wallet
and rings the front bell.
He looks through the narrow window beside the door.
The husband comes, finally,
checking his watch.

A Nice Town

Driving north on Highway 17,
she takes the bypass around Eunice.
That's a nice town, she thinks,
the trees and the post office, the Baptist church,
the Tiptoe Lounge.
She stops and gets out, lifts the town like flagstone
and puts it on the seat beside her.

I Describe to My Furniture a House I May Buy

My sofa wants it,
wants to dig into the carpet
its pig legs.
The dining table can't wait to tap
its toenails into the vinyl.
Every night they set up a clamor.
Buy it! Buy it!

I remind them
they've been wrong before.

A Bottomlands Farmer's Wife Speaks after Attempting Suicide

I know it is a sin.
But Lord I was tired. The older kids scraping in
and out of the trailer,
the steaming diapers,
the promise of checks he'll send.
Here come the police, driving like hell to catch their sirens.
When they stop,
they'll slam the shiny doors of their cars
hard as they can.
I used to dread that sound. I liked it too.
Like my mother's voice shouting me to come in
or else.

The Road

It is shorter, the trees lining it more sparse,
than when I went down it last.
The house at the end of it—
was it always that color?
And what happened to the glider
that used to sit on the porch?

A woman opens the screen door,
shutting it softly
the way I remember my grandmother doing.
The road lengthens. The trees lean toward each other
and touch.
The house is the right color;
in the glider on the porch
my uncle is rocking, reading *Forever Amber,*
refusing to tell me the story.

Driving Alone

An hour now
and not another car.
Sunset takes the light, the sound.
She reaches for the radio,
already on.

For All They Know

A man became bored with his children.
They brought him family photographs;
they asked him to tell the stories.

He told them nothing,
dreaming his life
as if they had never been.

He might have ferried camels over the world's
great deserts. Been a duffer in Spokane.
Danced in Salzburg with Garbo.
For all they know.

A Beginning

The couple coming to view the doublewide
tell themselves it looks like a house.
You can't hardly tell where they put it together, she says,
taking the man's arm. Look at the shutters.
It'll need paint, he says, walking closer,
putting on and taking off his cap.

The young salesman crossing the gravel lot
curses the heat, needing a cigarette.
He points out the size of the living room,
that the previous owners didn't have pets.

The woman sees herself putting up curtains.
She'll need to paper the bath. She'll ask the man
to build a deck, after work, on Sundays.
They'll get a dog, plant zinnias in the back.

The salesman ushers them into a steamy office.
He jokes, taking some papers out of a desk,
and a fat maroon pen. The man says
they might be back tomorrow, that he and the woman
will have to talk. But he sees her face is brighter
than sometimes when they make love, brighter even

than when they were married. He sits down with the salesman,
shuffling through the papers, not reading them,
seeing their bedroom in his mother's house
where his wife is spreading a shirt to iron.

He is afraid in a way he has never been.

Buzzards Near Osawatomie

Until one of them spread his wings
in front of the sun
like combs of translucent tortoise,
she didn't see the four of them,
black as the shed's black roof they perched upon.

When one floated down the side of the shed
to ease into shadows
where a door had been,
she wanted to go home,
marry the house and the children.

At Dark

Night falls at the open-air concert.
The stage is empty and dark.
Then the lone guitarist takes a step,
bringing with him the light.

In the front row,
bits of mirrors from a girl's dress
murmur like stories told from porches
as a mockingbird calls,
as green yards die into moonlight.

Seeing Her

A woman pilfering the dumpsters
in Monroe, Louisiana
sees dreams in the heat
that shimmers across the streets and bayous.
She knows what she needs:
A silky dress. Perfume.
Shoes with straps to tie at the ankle.
With these she might find
the man who, seeing her, can see
the columned house, the silver,
the deeply polished floors.

War Bride 1943

She's Betty Grable in platform shoes.
He's Dana Andrews.
She lights the candles and pours wine.
Everybody says
the war will be over soon.
The bride and her husband
drink to that.
From the radio, songs:
"Tea for Two," "Mairzy Doats,"
and "When the Lights Go On Again."
Closing the door behind them now,
they step out on the town.
When he ships out,
she'll go to stay with his mother
in Des Moines.

Baseball in America

It's what some of us still count on,
always in the background
desultory and insistent
like trains, or mothers.

The Suit

Awake, asleep,
the woman dreams a suit to its perfection:
red silk,
crisp peplum,
lining pink as a conch.

Imposters come. More will.
But the woman and the suit
wait for each other.
It burns to sit upon her shoulders,
to button itself firmly about her ribs.

She longs to give herself to it.
Its red will be the red of parrots.
It will fit like an old despair.
It will bite its beholders' eyes.

I Drive into a Town for the First Time

Wind wraps around a town
wrapped around a courthouse square.
The town's only bank
sits beside the town's only tree.
The customers of the East Side Café look up,
look up again
as I walk in and take a seat.
The faces are vaguely familiar,
the old names swimming a slow crawl
to meet them.
A man touches his cap and comes toward me—
Fred Simpson, how long has it been—
his smile meant for another table.

How Life Sometimes Is like Kansas

Think of yourself in a car
meeting an eighteen-wheeler
on a gray highway
under the bluest sky in America.
The ordinary clouds have all found their places.
You and the truck meet and pass
without a sound.
Think of fingers slammed in a car door,
of that moment
before the body is given notice.

Burying My Father

At the cemetery

the casket is taken out of the hearse
and placed carefully
before the disinterested chairs.

The preacher's words. The people.
Across the highway,
the reassuring hum

of a mowing machine.
I think of the other machine that will come
to put the coffin beside my mother's,

under the double stone.
Overhead
a knot of birds banks into the sun,

erasing itself.

A Great Plains Farmer Beseeches the Lord for Rain

We've come a long way from you, Lord,
a fact most of us acknowledge.
Sinners, all, but we do suffer.
The few trees left are shriven.
The ground divides and shifts,
a peril to dogs and children
and cattle worse off than Job's.
Everywhere about us, commandments break.

Elmer Brantlee's wheat dried up;
rumor has it the bank will foreclose.
I warrant it doesn't matter much
in the scheme of things. The radio
says rain. But who can believe?

I owe the bank more than I'll let on.
The wife, she's taken to smiling less:
there's no money now for those things she craves.

And there is this minor thing
a rain might ease:
She sleeps—because of the heat, she claims—
as far from me in bed as ever she can.

So, Lord . . . if I am just, and if you please.

Long Lives

In a small town
a man and a woman, evenings,
go out their separate garden gates
to take walks together,
to talk politics and roses and the way weeds can grow
on crocodiles' backs.
These are the ways they touch,
their voices falling and lifting
in the dark.

Dirt

2001

I.

Mockingbird

I sleep in my daughter's house.
The yard bristles with moonlight.
A mockingbird sings,
notes falling at the foot of a tree.

My daughter sleeps,
dreaming the voices of children
under her lids.
Her husband, a farmer, sleeps,
dreaming his fields.

I have nothing to bring to dreams.
The mockingbird and I are happy,
losing everything.

Telling Time

My son and I walk away
from his sister's day-old grave.
Our backs to the sun,
the forward pitch of our shadows
tells us the time.
By sweetest accident
he inclines
his shadow, touching mine.

Dirt

Its arrogance will break your heart.
Two weeks ago
we had to coax it
into taking her body.
Today,
after a light rain,
I see it hasn't bothered
to conceal its seams.

At a Daughter's Grave

It is Spring.
I hope the man planting in the next field
will stay close as he can to her
all day,
the tractor humming,
the diesel smoke
a constantly changing veil.

Why I Get Up Each Day

Tomorrow, maybe, or today
sunlight will discover one red leaf.
The sound will shatter crystal.

Crossing

One night, crossing a field,
I stepped through a skin of moonlight
like the one
found sometimes on milk.

I don't truck with moonlight anymore.
I sleep with the light on.
I've come to my senses.

Standing at a New Grave

In the midst of grief
the train,
wart-ugly, heartless as a toad.
I would like to shout my gratitude
as it crosses Old Cemetery Road
like a shock of rain,
blustering and insufferable and clean.

Houston

I have brought her here
too late.
The cancer has advanced.
There is nothing, the doctors tell us,
they can do.

As we drive back to our motel,
hundreds of grackles
in the ornamental trees
reel out their steely, flexible song
like the paper tongues of noise-makers we used to buy
for New Year's Eve.

Metaphor

After the coffin lid closes
over the body,
the silence
is sometimes described as noise.
It is not.
It is silence
and the mourners float upon it
like bathtub toys.

Indulgences

The bracelets were fourteen-karat,
a matched pair.
She bought them in Savannah
and wore them every day,
one on each wrist.

One summer she sold them
to pay back rent.

She remembers their every dent,
the light waffling over them,
the delicate guard chains swinging
as she walked.

Waiting for the dealer in New Orleans
to name a price,
she saw hundreds of pairs of gold bracelets,
some so small
she imagined them worn by blond children
playing on clipped lawns,
their parents smiling, looking on
as the children worried the chains to breaking
with their teeth.

Glittering

Some I consider wise
tell me
grief is best endured
when its edges fade,
when numbness follows disaster,
when you find
whatever safe house
time, in due time, will offer.

Once I might have agreed.
But I lost her.

Now I pray for torment,
that her glittering shapes
burn through my skin
to bone,
the wound a shifting pattern
that will not heal.

This Morning

As I drive into town
the driver in front of me
runs a stop sign.
A pedestrian pulls down his cap.
A man comes out of his house
to sweep the steps.
Ordinariness
bright as raspberries.

I turn on the radio.
Somebody tells me
the day is sunny and warm.
A woman laughs

and my daughter steps out of the radio.
Grief spreads in my throat like strep.
I had forgotten, I was happy, I maybe
was humming "You Are My Lucky Star,"
a song I may have invented.
Sometimes a red geranium, a dog,
a stone
will carry me away.
But not for long.
Some memory or another of her
catches up with me and stands
like an old nun behind a desk,
ruler in hand.

Kansas in Winter

The only thing alive in this landscape
is a woman filling her car with gas
at a 7-11,
unaware how important this drama is
against the farmhouses, their squares of glass dumb
against a sky empty of birds.

Weight

We are watching a PeeWee game.
My husband scrambles out of the bleachers
to get a Coke.
The space beside me where he had been
grows darker in the cooling dark.
When he returns,
the plank sags slightly
with his weight.
I want to sing.

II.

Summer

Every summer when I was a child,
I visited my grandmother's farm.
We didn't say much to each other,
listening to voices:
the far bark of a dog,
from somewhere, thunder,
the easy complaint
of the porch swing.

When it rains,
quickening old ashes in the fireplace,
I want to go back,
to the house that was,
the people that were,
the chores, the horses, the cat.

But what if I could?
What if someone,
glancing up from a sewing machine or a plow,
should see me there?

Piano

It was a Steinway baby grand,
clearly beyond our means.
I think when my mother sat down to play,
plunking down and picking up each note
as if it were concrete,
she was filling the corners
of that hardscrabble house she grew up in,
revising rooms with no music
not even a radio,
where, except for an occasional sparrow,
noon lay quiet as midnight.

Growing Up in a Small Town

Our fathers
kept the sky
from falling.
Our mothers,
talking of recipes and funerals
and that Hopkins girl,
wove our world.

North of Cabot

I think of my grandfather's rock-bitten farm,
crops burned to dust,
crows scolding him
from the barn.
Every time he took me to the baby's grave,
he spoke of the diphtheria.
Your grandmother never got over it, he said.
Too far from town
for any doctor.

An Old Woman Recalls a Sea Change

When I was six, she said,
every day was summer.
When I was seven, she said,
I stood at my mother's new-dug grave.
That night
I made supper for my father.
I swept each room.
I waited for him to speak.

In 1942

We had an enemy and a war
and neighborhoods that knew our names
and fathers smiling at us
from places found only on maps.

Once in a great while,
a package would come,
a jacket or a robe embroidered with a dragon
that nobody would let us wear.

For Stephen, Who Owns a Bag of My Cut Fingernails Carried in the Mouth of an Eel Who Swam the Caddo

On out fifteen miles past Wabbaseka,
past Seaton, Gethsemane, and Plain,
he and I grew up neighbors in houses
facing Danner's Bayou. White plantation houses,
splendid except for needing paint.

Except for occasional killings,
times were quiet.
One night the police broke into Mama Laura's place,
The Dew-Drop Inn on Third where the black people went.
They found where a fire had been, and bones.
She got the bones, they said, out of graves.
Then my grandfather told me about Vera,
who worked for my mother. He said that's where
they all learned.

We went to her place and hollered till she came out,
scraping the wash-house door.
We begged her to tell us. She told us no.
She said my mama would run her off,
and we were babies.
We were ten and twelve. We loved the way she smelled.
We wanted to know about the bones.
She said we were evil children.
She said to come back in an hour.

All through high school he and I met at the bayou,
early, before flies.
We tried to do what she'd taught us. We got scared.

One April morning in my senior year,
the moon in its last quarter,
we got it. Except neither of us knew the woman
we made appear.
We scraped the twigs together
and watched them burn.

I knew we had the power.
I said we ought to tell Vera,
who'd quit us and gone home.
She died in middle August, during drought.
Neighbors who went in for the body
found in the top of her closet
a little coffin
not much bigger than a shoebox,
with owls' feet and a few thin sticks.

He went to college in Missouri.
I buried Mama and went to work for the bank.
I wrote him drought was ruining Danner's Bayou.

We never got married. It seemed as though we would.
One day I came to be in St. Louis.
Gazing in a storefront, I saw his reflection
in back of mine.
No accident, he said. He caused it.

We often used the power after that.
That time we met in Bonn, that was my doing.
That time in Platte, as the traffic light changed.

It's two years since I saw him last.
Crossing a street in Memphis,
I enter a bar in Portland, Maine.
He is nowhere around.

I freeze to think what's happening in that bayou,
the three sticks crossing,
the owl dropping a stone where the sticks cross.
The awful joy of it. The tooth, the nail, the blazing.
Looking for him, I circle through the bar.
I look in a mirror.
The person I see does not have my face,
and backs away.

Kansas Town When the Sun Goes Down

Nebraska
hums on the horizon.

Parlors

We were the nieces, the daughters.
They were the uncles, the fathers. They
had keys
to houses, wives, offices,
to God.
After supper they jostled into the parlor
to smoke.
They lowered their voices
away from us.
They told us
part of the joke,
some of the story.

America

They said America would be
and it was:
the people, the parks,
the wars.

My mother and my father
said their life together would be
and it was:
the farm, the dog,
the dining table.

When I was five,
during the Great Depression,
there came in the mail one day
instructions for making a stand-up paper pig.
You started with an envelope.
The back of the pig
was one of the envelope's folds.

The envelope my mother brought me
seemed endless,
vast as a field of new snow.
I made the pig.

A Woman Remembers a Night

My husband turned off the headlights of the car
as we drove a deserted road one night,
the moon as large as the Sahara.

He was Rhett, escorting Scarlett,
both of us about to take
Atlanta, our house rich with silver
and spiral stairs.

He was a tenant farmer, working shares.
I cleaned for the landlord's wife.
As we drove up to the house,
chickens flew from the porch.

Boyfriend

We were both in high school, sixteen,
me headed for college.
They said he was bad.
They said his dad
was the one had bitten off the sheriff's ear
the night the sheriff came looking
for the still.

I'd hang around the gym
after the football team finished its practice,
hoping to see him.
I lied to my mother.

I saw a brightness, saw us dancing,
saw children who had his eyes.
Even now, I can smell the woodsmoke
in his jacket.

He never got out of the twelfth grade.
They said he went to work for the highway.
The girl he got pregnant was thirteen.
She wasn't from around here.

Hett Mayhew Explains Why Belton Harris Keeps His Sister Gladys Inside

Oftentimes they never know, Hett says.
It's likely Gladys never suspected
and couldn't understand what the fuss was
when the family found out
about the ears, the tail, the conversion
to three toes.

Hett says when a soul's possessed
a mirror breaks.
The soul becomes the soul of a beast
and the body starts to shape itself around it.
The shattered mirror can't show
how the hair grows to cover the face.

There are, however, clues:
Trees in the yard drop their leaves
out of season.
A shovel moves.
All the doors in the house
slam shut at noon.

Hett says you may notice that
and the cats with no tails
that come to your house on Tuesdays.
Or you may not.

Hett believes
Gladys Harris never noticed
and doesn't understand why she can't go out,
why somebody burned her shoes,

why a woman near the tracks in Pine Bluff
makes all her clothes.

A Good Woman

Some days all day she said nothing to us,
going early with her Bible to bed.
She was what they called
a good woman,
a name you earned
if your lips were fishing lines,
your hair the color of tin,
if every evening you rocked
waiting for his sour breath,
if as every hour was struck
you rocked harder
keeping one eye on the Bible and humming
if anyone entered the room—

if every night you prayed
for the cops and ambulance to come keening,
Agony and Pestilence
riding the sirens.

The Ferry

Whenever we needed to cross the Arkansas,
we had to take the dirt road to the ferry.
My father would drive.
My mother would fret
about missing the on-ramp,
driving off the other end,
getting caught by the dark.

After we bumped ourselves on
with a few other cars,
after the ferry coughed us away from shore,
the operator would shut the motor off
to drift as long as he dared.
Then we'd hear the motor again,
arguing with the current.

Thus we kept our course—
the river suffering us,
the sun easing down,
darkness closing over us
merciless as water.

Smoke

Every year in the fall of the year
the hoboes, the same ones, came
scrabbling out of dusty nowhere
to harvest rice on my father's farm.

Then, in the fall that I turned sixteen,
my father changed to machines to farm with.
We never saw the hoboes again.
I remember one: a lanky artist

who shyly one day sketched for me
his idea of home. In hesitant charcoal
a roof took shape, a door, a chimney,
tieback curtains, a curl of smoke.

I imagined the kitchen's sunny cat,
the kettle, the stove, the bowl of flowers.
The person who knew to draw me that
was what I had been wanting. But how

could I have known—disdainful, already turned,
dancing toward Joey Hawkins down the road.

Kissing

One scene from my childhood:
Spending the night at my Aunt Eva's,
I have come downstairs at midnight
for a glass of milk.
She and her husband, Ferdinand,
sit at the kitchen table, their backs to me.
His left trouser leg
is rolled up to his thigh.
The stump of the leg he lost under a tractor
is propped on a stool,
gleaming in the lamplight.
My aunt and uncle bend above it,
laughing uncontrollably and kissing.

Going Back

My father's fields lie empty.
My mother's crape myrtles
have died in their sleep.
Daring the abandoned steps,
I enter the farmhouse
and my old room.

Summer evenings,
I used to open these windows
to the sound of a mockingbird,
the moon creaking up
like a stage set.

In the silence
a wasp bumps its way
along the ceiling.

III.

Ties

It's late.
The mice in the walls have begun again.
The crickets have thinned
to a readable noise.
You look up from leafing a magazine
and say something woven out of our years together,
something only the two of us
would find amusing.
I think of this moment
as an incredible moth.
I want to keep it.

Having Just Met

They slip away from the party.
He touches her arm, finding a memory there.
A train begins its noise across Missouri.
She brushes a thread from his sleeve.

Threads

She had lost her memory at thirty-five.
"So what?" her husband always says, and smiles
when someone remarks. Tonight they've come
to hear B.B. King in concert, live, in Memphis.
They saw B.B. last year, but she can't recall.
Her husband reminds her of that evening now,
quickly moving them through the smoky crowd
so she can get a closer look. In perfect
patience and love, he seats her where she commands
a clear view of the stage, closing his hand
and opening it on the smooth back of her chair.
At the small table, their elbows touch.
On the stage, B.B. is resplendent in black
and baby blue. The husband asks his wife
if she remembers the color of the jacket
when they saw him last. "Pink," she says.
It was orange. But he likes the way she touches his arm
when memory skims the surface of her mind
like, he imagines, the shadow of a gull
over sleeping water. His face burns
with the thought, the hope, that tonight in bed—
perhaps early, perhaps late—she will turn
to him and speak against his back, recalling
the jacket perfectly.

Love Story

She confesses her love
for a man with a bald spot.
In summer the sun plays a one-note fortissimo upon it.
In winter it ices over.
She scatters suet on it.
Grackles sweep down.
She puts up a scarecrow for it
and a little canopy against the sleet.
Then they strut down the sidewalk together
like sleek, oiled crows.

What panoply! What noise!
The grackles clattering on the bald spot,
the magpies circling for the glint.

It's October now. First signs of sleet.
She tells him what she wants:
She wants to become a grackle,
beak and foot.

At Dusk

A woman stands behind a farmhouse
in Kansas.
Soothing her skirt,
the woman leans into the wind.
The wind takes
some of the zinnias
out of the pocket of the skirt.

A man walks toward her,
coming in from the fields.
Distance dances around them
like sheets of dust.

In Passing

When they were married.
Listen, he said.
I've made a deal.
We're moving to Greece.
Ah, she said. Well.

When the child was born.
Listen, he said.
We'll name him Peele.
After my niece.
Well, she said. Ah.

When the child went to school.
Listen, he said.
He's learned to steal.
They've called the police.
Ah, she said. Well.

When the child married.
Listen, he said.
The baby's due.
The baby's dead.
Well, she said. Ah.

When she left him.
Listen, she said.
There's milk in the fridge,
and figs and bread.
Also a stew.
Listen, he said.
Please.

She Returns to Remind Him How It Was When It Was Good between Them

She has powers. She doesn't use a door.
She enters like smoke,
like sunlight through a cat's ear.

He looks up.
"I never wanted to see you again. Ever."
Still, when she inclines her head like that . . .
Something he says makes her laugh.
He feels clever.
"Well," he says. "We'll see."

Courtly Love

A woman walks along Teche Bayou
with a man she loves.
A warm May evening.
He brings back for her a world
where her father wore a felt fedora
every day to work,
where her mother changed into a fresh dress
each afternoon.

The man touches her elbow.
Overhead, mimosas steep themselves
in bloom.

The Breakup

It's likely that the cause of it
wasn't any one thing,
certainly not anything
either one of them would believe.
Just the wearing away,
water constantly reminding stone.

At the Azure Sky Motel

Slowly, checking his tie in the mirror,
he says what he is almost sure
will end it.
His words taste to her like the dust she recalls
from the seats of her grandfather's
second-hand Buick.

Trying to remember
where she left her car,
she walks by the pool.
The voices of children
fly at her like birds,
sassy and useless.

After Supper

She liked the anger in her husband's eyes,
the moment of danger as she hurled the vase.
The vase fell childlike, fragile as prayer
or dusk as it waits to enter the tall grass.
Then the noise, bright and upright as pain.
When her husband spoke into the silence
the way he always did, she knew her lines.

A Second Cup of Coffee

According to their custom, Sundays,
a husband and wife exchanged the classifieds
and front page.
Pouring their second cups of coffee,
she told him she'd found out about the woman.
She placed and replaced her cup in the ring
it had made on the table.

They talked until the woman
became a name,
until how it began, and when,
advanced to a day and a street.

After she left,
taking the children with her,
he walked through rooms
not noticing,
forgetting where he had left his drink.

At dusk
he watched the mailbox,
the jonquils, the neighbor's elm
fall to the dark.
Only the white-blooming dogwood held
against it awhile.

Estate

They are talking in bed, late,
about their scheduled flight to the Bahamas.
Quietly, he says he guesses they ought to think about
their wills.

The way he says it, she thinks,
he might be suggesting they clean the basement.
What he proposes,
beneficiaries, executor,
a trust,
is logical, she guesses,
and sounds fair for the children.

On the radio someone is singing
"I've Got a Gal in Kalamazoo, Zoo, Zoo,"
a song they both remember from before the war.
Through the curtains comes a flicker of light,
someone turning into a driveway.
Her husband is suddenly asleep.
She tries to imagine.

IV.

The Good Hand

After a stroke of luck, my son's left hand
and arm lie lifeless. He has to remind
them, wherever he goes, to come along.
With the good hand he gives his old, strong

handshake, pulls on his shoes, adjusts his braces,
cooks, turns pages, touches the bored faces
of three dogs, struggles with rubber bands,
writes checks, drives a tractor, harrows and plants.

He caresses the hair of his two boys and his wife
and often takes with his good hand, my hand
or touches my shoulder when I sigh or laugh
over some loss we both can understand.

Evening

From a wood beyond the fields,
something dark has not yet advanced
toward the trimmed light
of the kitchen.
A woman puts away dishes.
A man goes through the mail.
A child leans over the table,
saying her homework.

The dog looks up once and growls
as if not meaning to, a sound
almost inaudible.
He clicks across the floor, nosing for crumbs.

In the Office of a Leading Oncologist

The potpourri can't overcome
the dread smell rising in this room.
Here, the spunky, inseparable twins,
diagnosis and prognosis, grin
to escort the hapless to their graves.
Thin as a prisoner, one waves
absently. Some sleep. One,
bald as a cricket, squints in the sun.

As if a book, chapter and verse
fell open, I see: the Angel with spurs
like knives in her wings waits here.
Here is the abyss. What else shall I fear?
There is no balm in Gilead, nor slumber.
No Rose of Sharon. No sainted number.

Truth is freedom but the noose is tightening.
The nurse calls my name.

Doves

At first, he thought little of it,
two doves on a ledge
under the window
of his wife's hospital room,
their movements fluid as iridescence,
as he waited with the kin
he'd called to come.

Later,
he saw that one of the doves was gone.
The one that remained
stood lusterless,
dismissed,
a stone.

Taking Chemotherapy

As it drips,
she thinks of herself
beside a trucker,
howling down an interstate.
Or fast dancing,
highest heels and briefest skirt,
her hair feathering against his cheek.

But that's one of her other selves,
the one who comes now
to sit beside her
and prattle about such things.

Waiting Room

I see you here most every day. How are you?
The coffee's gone. I've asked the desk for more
but I guess they're overworked and underpaid.
The nurses try. They've sure been good to us.
Who do you have here? I'm so sorry.
He's young, your son, isn't he, for that to happen?
Our son's here, too. He's not doing good. It's AIDS.
That was my husband that just left. He hates
for me to talk to anyone about Tommy.

Lord, it's expensive, having somebody here.
We're staying in our son's trailer. I'm afraid
he'll never go back to it. He's failed a lot
these last few days. How's your son? Well.
I'm so sorry. I'll be praying for him.

We live two hundred miles away. The driving
back and forth, we can't afford it. But even
staying in the trailer, you've got to eat,
and groceries are out of sight. We're getting too old
to drive in traffic. My husband doesn't do good
in places like this—the waiting, you know. Of course
you do. Does your son have children? Well,
there's no explaining these things. We take what comes.

I'm just thankful we can be here with Tommy.
You can't just walk away. Some do, you know.
Some of our friends said we ought to put
our son right out in the street. They would. My husband's
taking this real hard. He's aged ten years.
We've gone through nearly all our savings. I'm sure

you've noticed I'm missing some front teeth. Now,
I guess, I'll never get my partial plate.

I wish I could go buy me a new dress.
Might cheer Tommy up. He takes it hard
when I leave. All we can do is be here.
You can't just walk away. Remember, Hon,
we're all right where we're supposed to be.

That's what I tell my husband. Here he is.

Herschel, come and meet someone. Her son
is in here, too. I simply can't believe
that traffic. I've lived my whole life in this state
and never been, not once, in this city.
We had our boy late, a good baby,
never any trouble at all. You have to go?

God bless. One day at a time, that's what I say.
Will you be here tomorrow? If there's a miracle,
we'll have hot coffee. But I wouldn't hold my breath.

How to Imagine How It Will Be When the Doctor Comes Out to Say

Think of a man in Holland
the moment he sees a first break in the dike.
Think of Anne Frank at the moment she recognizes
the sound on the stair.

In No Time

He follows the doctor out of his father's room.
"Without treatment, he'll be gone
in no time."
"With treatment?"
"A few months, maybe. It's hard to tell."
He thanks the doctor and says the family
will talk.

Taking the elevator down, he tries to remember
everything the doctor said.

Crossing the parking lot,
he hears a high and shifting V of geese.
He turns up his collar.

In a Neck of the Woods

for John Downey

The woods are dense in the remote county
where a man has disappeared.
Despite a desperate search,
there is no trace.
His wife told authorities
her husband left, alone,
to camp overnight.
She said he was dressed, as always,
in black from head to foot.
Perhaps, after dark and before the moon rose,
the man went for firewood.

Perhaps, falling in step beside him,
night assumed the man's shape,
easing perfectly
into his shoes.

Grace

Seeing my grandchildren,
taking them in my arms,
I sometimes think it possible
to dance before the throne of God,
make small talk with Him,
my every jot and tittle of sin
forgiven.

Cancer

It eased under the door
like a mouse.
We scarcely noticed.
Then the scuttling.
Then the high squeak
that shattered the house.

Inheritance

A man dies,
leaving a farm and the house they grew up in
to his children,
who have married and moved away.
Indian summer brittles the fields.
Snow falls in the orchard.
The fields, the house, the tractor
shimmer and fade.

The children hire a lawyer
to settle everything.
Behind the windows of the house,
darkness and dust.

At Summer's End

A man calls his dog
at two a.m.
He whistles casually, as if to say
It's just a dumb dog.

The moon, a spider,
lets itself slowly down.

The man thinks of autumn.
He whistles again.

V.

Tempting the Muse

Tilt your head provocatively,
round your vowels,
make a place for him
in the cleavage of your breasts.
Hope for the best.
What you'll get is anybody's guess.

Once, I pulled out all the stops
and a pickpocket wandered in,
reeking of booze and need;
and once, Death,
who apologized for getting the wrong house
and went on his way—
but not before his eyes,
red as a red snapper's,
undid every button of my dress.

Who Could Ask for Anything More

Every Saturday
somebody in a cat costume
stands in the parking lot
across from my apartment,
hustling for the Mew-Mew Groom and Board.

His white fur needs a bath. One ear
is wrong.
There's a hole in his paw.

Although he dutifully waves to all who pass,
I have never seen anyone
wave back.
Or stop to leave a cat.

Staring out the window,
I picture the two of us together.
I know his hands and his face.
Yesterday we raked leaves.
Today, maybe we'll make
a pot of soup.

Intersection

I set up my ironing board at an intersection
so as not to impede traffic.
I sprinkled a shirt to slight dampness,
rolled it into a ball
and waited hours,
as my mother had taught me.

Just as every thread was moist
but before mildew attacked,
I spread the shirt, damp and inviting,
on the board.

A musty steam arose
as the point of my iron touched the collar.

A man stopped his car to chat,
honking his horn.
Many interested people
leaned out of their cars.

On the Brink

for Tony Beasley

A boy, a week away
from graduating high school,
is taken to dinner
by his father's oldest friend.
The brandies cleared,
the man removes from the cuffs of his shirt
a pair of eighteen-karat, ruby-studded cuff links
the boy has long admired.
He hands them to the boy
who tonight, for the first time,
confronts the stench
of circumstance and good luck.

The Phenomenological World

As I drive by my neighbor's yard,
a swan I've mistaken daily for an ornament
raises a wing.

Gratitude

Sometimes it's a species of titmouse,
a wart hog,
a parrot who fancies himself a dandy,
can change your life.

A man in Ohio lost his wife
because a parrot they'd bought in Tahiti
slipped his cage.
The parrot's name was Starley.
The cage was papered in white snake.

When the parrot left, the wife left.
"Life without Starley," she said, "is a bubbleless champagne."

The man sold the Rolls and the houses.
He moved into the cage.
There he writes his autobiography,
which will come out in the spring
and contains a dedication to the parrot
who, rumor has it, keeps a house and a boy
in Deauville.
The dedication reads
"To Starley. Who made it all possible.
With eternal gratitude, Bill."

Across Town

A woman spends the morning in juvenile court
with her son.
She sees him handcuffed and taken.
She goes home to a stifling house,
no trees in the yard.

Across town
under giant elms,
to the mild disinterest of the family cat,
a boy the same age as the woman's son
is lazily catching lizards.

Privilege

I see them in Wal-Mart.
She is a round-faced madonna,
a little on the beefy side
but sweet-faced, reminding me of days in June,
and crickets and water over stones.
He is bearded, going a trifle bald,
his face too large for the body
which has shrunk away.
His arms and legs
dangle like a rag doll's
as she carries him on his back in her arms.
Amazed, wondering what awful disease,
everyone stares.

A younger woman,
her hair falling from several crooked parts
like onion sets, strolls beside them.
The two children she offers up to Santa
howl as if they had been struck.
The group heads for Toys through Housewares,
the man and madonna smiling at each other
as she strokes his knee.

Walking to my car, I take out my wallet
to touch the snapshots
under the milky plastic.
My dead mother squints at me,
twisting her rings. My son,
splendid in tie and suit,
stands against solid mahogany.

The Order of Things

I tell a grandchild young enough
to care about it
how I discovered a chipmunk one afternoon
in a nearby field.
It was so well camouflaged, I said,
that I almost didn't see it.
What made you see it?
It moved.
Why did it move?
To find something to eat.
Then I told him about the hawk.

Mercy

The night after his two children burned
in a frame house in a searing drought,
the man, the neighbors said,
wandered through his yard
murmuring "Lord have mercy."
And the Lord sent rain.

Luck

In the middle of phoning in an order
to Spiegel,
a woman discovers
she's been struck dumb.
When the doctors tell her there is no cure,
she smiles. If she could, she would tell them
her joy.
She remembers a time when she was a child,
pinning towels on the line
in the white and sparkling silence of
the farm.

The Night Clerk at L. L. Bean

for Huey Crisp

His phone rings almost all night,
as measured and intense
as somebody smoking a cigarette.
Taking an order for a monogrammed dog bed,
he remembers the time
a fox watched him, motionless,
from the edge of a field.

This is sometimes how grace comes to us,
sharp and fleeting as a paper cut.

Holes

A woman showed her dry cleaner
the minute holes in a wool suit.
"When do they hatch?" she demanded.
"These moths lay their eggs, they hatch,
and what is hatched
eats holes in my good wool.
When? What time of year?"
She riveted her voice
into the eyes of the man who owned
O.K. and Milady Dry Cleaners.

The man looked down, folding the suit
like a pair of socks.
He told her to come back Friday.

The woman leaned over the counter.
"You don't know the first thing
about moths."

Until she died,
the woman spent one night a week
burning holes in her jackets and skirts,
burning the baby merino, the cashmere, alpaca,
gabardine, the serge.

She liked the fear on the man's face
when she came into his shop each Friday
with an armload of clothes.

Scorch

After a summer flood
consumed the forty acres of soybeans
and all but the roof of her house,
the woman who lived there
went back. The trees around the fields
were marked by a line so even
it might have been computer-drawn.
Above the line, the trees were green;
below it, brown without nuance.
Where the water and dirt had lingered
above the topmost windows,
the white two-storied house bore
a band as dirty as scorch.

Seeing that, the woman's breasts ached
as if she had lost a child.
She ordered scaffolding built,
and a catwalk to surround the house.
One night, climbing on the catwalk,
touching the house,
she felt the breath of what had been there—
vases and raincoats and dogs and shoes.

She knew what she must do.
Addressing the band that shone in the moonlight,
she walked the circumference of the house,
licking it clean.

What We Need

It is just as well we do not see,
in the shadows behind the hasty tent
of the Allen Brothers Greatest Show,
Lola the Lion Tamer and the Great Valdini
in Nikes and jeans
sharing a tired cigarette
before she girds her wrists with glistening amulets
and snaps the tigers into rage,
before he adjusts the glimmering cummerbund
and makes from air
the white and trembling doves, the pair.

Satisfied with Havoc

2004

I.

Stranger

New in town,
I'm sitting at the counter in Marge's Grill,
hiding behind a magazine,
reading about a man whose job is stitching corpses
in a funeral home.
The talk around me is of rain,
if it won't or will,
a losing Little League,
the farm show.

I think of the farm I grew up on,
the one nobody here would know;
the clarity of the moons,
quartered or halved or full,
hauling themselves up from behind the sheds.

In a dazzling moment of estrangement,
I leave my money on the counter,
cool to my touch.

Married

Tonight I ask my husband to help me remember
names for the breeds of chickens
he and I grew up with, living on neighboring farms.
From the far, tall grasses he calls them:
    Wyandottes. Dominiques. Barred Rocks.
    Rhode Island Reds. Silver Spangled Hamburgs.
    Leghorns. Anconas. Buff Orpingtons . . .
"Mother used to call them 'Buff Orphans,'" I interrupt.
We laugh. He remembers my mother.
Evening settles itself,
whispering snow.
The kitchen nightlight makes a tiny moon
on the wall.

After Losing a Child

A man and a woman sit on the deck
in afternoon light.
She pushes back her chair.
He moves closer to catch her voice.
Dusk leafs absently through the trees.
They listen to whippoorwills
stitch and unstitch the same seam
in the dark.

Watching a Grandson Play Little League Ball
the Day Ted Williams Died

for Merritt

It is late afternoon.
All over America, this scene:
distant traffic, the sound of the evening train,
parents calling out their children's names.

Mothers and Daughters

When I was a child,
my mother and I traveled the long miles
to see her mother, once a year.
That hillside farm was mostly gravel,
the kitchen smelled like a churn,
guineas and chickens strutted the porch.
When we left,
my grandmother would stand
in her garden and wave.
I'd watch her a long time,
leaning out the window of the car.
My mother would say little on the way home,
her eyes now and then filling with tears.
Perhaps she was thinking of that garden,
the one she tried to replicate year after year,
every last pole bean and zinnia,
the one she left to me.

At Frog's Trailer Park

The three p.m. August heat
seeps under the cars,
whipping the dogs,
baking the trailers
like loaves of bread.

A woman using the park's public phone
wipes away the sweat,
fixing her eyes on a spot just above the asphalt
where for her, perhaps, the heat assumes
a familiar shape—a turtle, say, or a heron.
The heron might be blue,
standing in cool water.

Silence

for Barry Strauss

Older in these winter days,
I yearn less and less for silence.
I welcome the faucet's protest
in the room above mine,
the heavy tread of someone
late perhaps to work.

I look out on a meadow.
The deer, where are they?
It is not enough to see their tracks,
where they wandered yesterday.
I need the flick of their bodies
snapping a twig,
the chuff of their breath.

The sun slips down,
reluctant to disappear,
the way sound dims a room
when we turn off a radio.

Work

for Miller and Jordan Williams

It is summer, dusk.
Sitting with your wife on the lawn,
you think of the day's work you have done,
how you lowered yourself into it slowly,
as a coffin might enter a grave.
Work is good, the crickets promise.
The cicadas agree.
The worm makes no noise,
busy about its chiseling.
In the sudden quiet,
the faint scratch of hooves—
as if a horse you'd known as a child
were cantering round a nearby field.

Your heart settles itself
like moon upon water
as you regard the dark,
the work yet to be done,
the woman beside you.
Against a blackening sky,
fireflies dim.

The House on Lake Ice Road

Sunlight jimmies its way
through the dusty windows.
On the kitchen table
one orange leans against the blue sky of a bowl
where someone has dropped a mitten,
keys, a greasy sack.
My friend pours the coffee;
I clear a space for the cups.
I want this never to change.
The clock (Big Ben, red hands, 1930s plastic)
dutifully erases our every word.

The Wait

A buzzard riding the thermals
above a pine beside a Louisiana highway
spots the carcass of a small dog
left by a speeding car.
It is mid-July. A gossamer of trembling
alerts the buzzard's spine.
Here is an odor with promise.
Soon the air will turn to an oily shimmer,
a texture of such velvet and exquisite heft
that the buzzard contents himself to wait,
rocking night after night in the arms of the pine.

Paying Attention

Coming home to visit my parents' graves,
I enter the house where I was born.
My mother sits at a table, sewing,
her eyes a deepening blue.
My father comes in from the fields.
Until now I have never known
that intent young man,
that slender woman
who lean toward each other
and touch hands
and rise together to climb the stairs,
long vistas of the fields dissolving
as dusk puts down its roots.

Honeymoon

On their way home from the honeymoon
("fantastic weekend, heart-shaped tub,
breathtaking views"),
they stop at a run-down motel.
She hadn't realized he'd be so
economical.
She hopes there's more than one towel,
that the sheets are clean,
that he won't say the things, as he did last night,
to make her cry,
things not unlike
what her father used to say to her mother
as she listened from the dark of the stairs.

Sometime in the night
she hears a woman sobbing in the next room.
Moonlight papers the walls.
She thinks of every ramshackle house
her father moved them in and out of.

Just before sleep,
she glimpses herself in a far corner,
brushing her hair,
rehearsing something she'll say at first light
to make her husband make a fist.

Snow

When God created snow,
He melted down coyote, wolf,
eagle, wolverine, fisher, fox
into a darkness
that falls when it chooses,
decked out in trickster white,
that tracks us,
curious and aloof,
wanting a key,
a scarf,
breath.

The Aunts

for Victor Girerd

In Charleroi, Belgium,
they stand in front of the family home,
arms linked,
as someone takes this photograph
dated 1952.
They are three:
Amelia, a spy for the resistance,
imprisoned by the Germans in World War I;
Augusta, my father's mother,
who ran away to America at seventeen;
Marie, who helped her in that deceit.

These years later,
defiant in smart hats and suits,
they study me,
clearly disappointed.

Walking in Woods

Lift the forest floor, slightly.
Be aware of what is hiding,
going about its business
in the silky chambers of itself.
And should that creature shyly one day
come to you,
or a bird cut out a song from the papery sky
and float it toward you,
think it neither by your cunning
nor your grace
that the world happened to tip its hat—a lilt, a shadow—
as you happened to pass.

On That Beautiful Shore

Last night, alone in the kitchen,
I felt my dead mother brush my sleeve.
She wasn't smiling. She didn't say
How are you, How are the kids?
She was, I have to say it, rude.
Talking to the dead,
you can't be sure they hear.
You tell yourself they do,
that they're merely distracted,
doing their best to fit in
to the sweet bye and bye.

You wonder if it's hard to make friends there,
if now that they're nothing but air
they stumble over things,
how they cope with never saying words
like *foxglove* or *nasturtium* again.

The Slight

From the wooded swale
behind the house,
the last of the snow
has come to die,
ghosts of it rising,
sifting north along a ridge.

Although they've ventured perilously close,
it's clear they have no use for us,
nodding among themselves,
turning their backs,
going about their business.

We, too, return to our tasks—sorting potatoes,
mending a sock—
miffed and oddly out of sorts.

Driving Highway 71

Gliding into sleep,
I caught myself just before crossing
the center line.
At that moment a hawk,
alert to something on the highway,
dove perilously close to my left wheel.
As he corrected,
as sunlight powered his decision,
I saw at my left hand
the silver underside of his wing.

Shouldn't there have been cymbals,
a crescendo of sound?
A sea had parted to let us pass,
closing behind us
with scarcely a flicker.

To My Daughter, Who Refuses to Meet Me Halfway

As implacable as my mother's garden
jelled in moonlight,
as silent as the dog who disappeared forever
down a dusty lane,
the dead remain estranged.
Daily they recede,
seeking the more distant stars.

Dating our lives from their departures,
we beg them for signs.
We want to stumble upon them napping
or peeling an orange.
They send nothing, no nearer to us now
than the day they nodded to Death
and asked him in.

Dumb

You would think the dog,
lemon-sized brain notwithstanding,
would understand by now
that the truck with the broken muffler
passing down our street each night
is not his master's truck
and will not turn into our driveway;
the familiar key will not undress itself
in our lock.
Still, he bounds to the door
at the muffler's first faint cough.
Thus hope outfoxes reason,
the dog and I growing dumber by the week.

II.

The Crows of Mica Street

Their calls grate
like shears cutting heavy tin.
Misfits among the robins and wrens,
they flock to this street,
stolid as midwives on their rounds.
I receive their song in my ruined life
like scalding water in a new wound.
I walk on, redeemed.

Straightpins

Growing up in a small town,
we didn't notice
the background figures of our lives,
gray men, gnarled women,
dropping from us silently
like straightpins to a dressmaker's floor.
The old did not die
but simply vanished
like discs of snow on our tongues.
We knew nothing then of nothingness
or pain or loss—
our days filled with open fields,
football,
turtles and cows.

One day we noticed
Death has a musty breath,
that some we loved
died dreadfully,
that dying
sometimes takes time.

Now, standing in a supermarket line
or easing out of a parking lot,
we realize
we've become the hazy backgrounds
of younger lives.
How long has it been,
we ask no one in particular,
since we've seen a turtle
or a cow?

New Couple on the Block

We give them a week
to settle in.
We ask them over to a neighborhood buffet.

She is talkative; he is aloof.
Over dessert, someone asks him
"What is it you do?"
He says he builds houses.
He says the last one was made
of pink corrugated cardboard,
surrounded by a moat.
Landscaped, of course.
The men murmur politely
and study their plates.

I look at our guest.
He's leaning back,
savoring his wine.
I think I understand
how he survives.

Pristine

It's what we want—
the antique's impeccable provenance,
the surround smell of the new car,
sheets just out of the wash.
In this room
the walls are white,
waiting for the moon.
I think of the city I have left,
its sirens, its Wal-Marts,
its viper streets.
Looking out into woods
that take scarce note of this window,
I think of caribou
crossing first snow.

Cloud's Lake

The summer Sammy Erickson drowned
we were fifteen, immortal.
When we heard they couldn't find the body,
we buried his memory
like a contentious bone.
We knew the lake he'd drowned in;
it was our silvery world.
We laid our blankets down beside it,
built small fires and counted stars.
We ignored the razors of glass
nightly sharpening themselves along the shore,
the stuttering codes
glinting off the water.
Picnics, white sails, our young bodies
obscured the docks' slow rot,
stumps rising under speeding boats
like sharks,
the bones of Sammy Erickson
turning the wrong way home.

Snow in a New Hampshire Spring

with a tip of the hat to James Dickey

Snow, my boon companion,
my rock of ages,
my delight, my destroyer,
my church, my foundation—
who has redeemed the earth
and swept away the stench of dead leaves—
you are shrinking, melting
down to your grave.
Even now
you succumb to the grass
storming the hill,
its young and ignorant body
wild to take everything.

The Boys from Brewer Bottoms

Coach Danner loved them.
With those boys on the team
our high school won All-District in football
every year.
Coach never told them what to do. They knew.
They'd grown up
defending their fathers' stills.
They knew every shortcut in those swamps and woods
to outfox the sheriff and his dogs.
The town doctor said
when he was sent for by one of them
somebody would meet him at the highway
and take him in by boat.
They always made sure
he saw the rifle.

We heard they lived in shacks and ate snakes.
We heard all strangers disappeared
without a trace.
On the football field
envy and moonshine drove their brains.
They hated the town boys,
whose fathers worked
and drank coffee every morning
with the sheriff and the chief of police.
They were handsome and polite,
respected their elders,
could crack a man's back,
their blue eyes smiling.

Taken

Doing battle with the fly swatter and the Raid,
I stun the red rambunctious wasp
cavorting in my den.
It stutters and simmers. It grows still.
Remorse sets in.
What if I, dancing one night
alone in my room,
should catch the ever-roving eye of God
and be struck down,
dispatched like a gnat,
God being God and marginally annoyed?

Flying over the Scablands, Seattle to Pullman

for Paula Coomer

As we climb,
I see a glass lake,
a desert marked with dead waves,
dots of forests
green as astroturf.

If we go down,
we may fall into those cardboard trees,
those scablands thin as snakeskin,
that bored lake
which may or may not extinguish
our inconvenient flames.

A Bottomlands Farmer Remembers a Ball-Peen Hammer

He was the master of it, my father was,
killing snakes with it, battening shingles down,
threatening the convicts the prison sent him, summers,
to pull Johnson grass out of the fields.
It wasn't the hammer made me afraid that day
when, spitting my name, he came at me,
stopping himself as he drew back his arm—
his knuckles white as gristle
as he threw the hammer down,
his eyes rid of me forever.

A Woman Tires of Hearing Acorns on the Roof

All October they have dinged our roof
like berserk goats.

Today my doctor has phoned.
The tests have come back positive;
he'll see me in his office
tomorrow.

Hungry now for snow to lay down
its quiet tarpaulins,
I recall the dirt I was instructed to scatter
as a child, how it rang
on my grandfather's lowered coffin.

Dance

in memory of Agha Shahid Ali

Shahid would say, if he had lived to see
another spring,
A bird on a far ridge
recalling how a song is sung,
the tap dances of mice
between the walls,
the thickening air of fireflies
and flies—
Why not be happy?

The tulips and jonquils,
begonias and lilies—
upstarts of color,
arrogant shills,
silly to the core—
the petulant ambulance
which has not yet turned
down my street—

Come dance with me.

History

Our parents told us stories
from the Great Depression:
my father's mother hiding her last dollar
in the garden
under the second plant
in the second row of spinach,
my mother's cousin
found hanged by his Sunday necktie
in the kitchen
after the factory laid him off.

These stories bumped our lives
like old-maid aunts coming to visit—
exotic, worrisome, finally gone—
while our parents struggled to provide us
with packaged bread,
clean underwear,
sidewalks lined with pink and purple phlox.

Balance

After you're gone,
after the children have rifled through your things,
the papers and paperweights,
the policies and pewter pigs,
all will be factored in,
deducted from your balance—
how you took ten photos of one grandchild
at Christmas
and only five and two of the others,
the letters you forgot to burn—
and, to your credit, your request
that equal numbers of the Sunday dishes
go to everyone.

Then the children will return to their lives
slighted and scorned,
arguing for years
over who should get this button,
that cracked comb.

Blackbird

It's been over forty years.
On a monotonous highway in November rain
the car in front of me
vanished and entered the world again
upside down in a field.
A man and a woman lay in the stubble wheat.

    As if in a movie,
    I see myself kneel beside them
    to cover the woman with my coat.
    They say nothing, staring at the sky.
    The *kong-ka-ree, kong-ka-ree* of a red-winged blackbird
    rings out;
    then I hear the silence.

Memory brightens the scene that day
when the world shattered in a breath—
my yellow coat against the brown field,
the trickle of red from the woman's lips,
the gray and distant trees,
the blackbird, its crimson epaulets,
the song that came to live in my brain
and has never slept.

Tarantula

Walking the dog,
I see an out-of-round paper cup
wobbling like a tarantula
down the hill.

I am five.
My grandmother's voice fills the world.
"Get back! Get back!" she shouts
as a black shape advances over the rocks.
Later she tells me the spider's name.

Longing dumbfounds me: that house, those rocks, her face,
the bowl with the one wax pear
catching dust on the kitchen table.

Mammogram

"They're benign," the radiologist says,
pointing to specks on the x ray
that look like dust motes
stopped cold in their dance.
His words take my spine like flame.
I suddenly love
the radiologist, the nurse, the paper gown,
the vapid print on the dressing room wall.
I pull on my radiant clothes.
I step out into the Hanging Gardens, the Taj Mahal,
the Niagara Falls of the parking lot.

Taxidermy

Let us mourn the giraffe and zebra,
dead during heavy bombardment
in a Gaza Strip zoo—
one of terror,
one of tear gas.
There is no money to replace them,
so they will be stuffed
and put back in their cages
for children to see
how it was when these were animals—
although someone who can remember
will have to explain
how the brusque tails sent flies reeling;
how, like barley in an evening wind,
they bent their necks to water;
how the eyes were not glass then,
and darker.

III.

In the Critical Care Waiting Room

in memory of Ray and Mary Faver

The next of kin live in the green befores:
before the fall, the stroke, the mugger's knife,
cancer's knavery, the clot, battered doors
of the heart. Hope, doctors, strategies for buying
time consume their lives. They despise the blood,
tubes, smells, each day's descent into hell—
while a soft rain, the notes of a thrush
remind them spring is rising somewhere else;
somewhere someone is dancing a tango. They lose
keys, cars, good jackets, mail; make lists
and forget them; smile for the stricken father, spouse,
child; try not to think of the apocalypse.
In waiting they find order, all order gone,
their porch lights at noon burning absently on.

Strangers in This City Where We Have Come Seeking a Cure for Her Cancer, My Daughter and I Drive Up to the Clinic

A buzzard lands on the roof.
In the dusk, in my confusion,
I mistake it for a blue
heron. I call to my daughter, "Look!"

Coma

In this place
even your name won't keep you
from being anonymous.
When the nurse comes in,
I list your attributes:
witty, smooth dancer,
devoted to the dog.
Look, I want to shout. This is my friend.
This is who he is.
I take from my wallet your photograph
in the absurd blue tux.
The nurse nods politely,
but her eye is on the sparrows
of your chart,
drab waves and dots.

You lie lost,
your blood turned to shadow.
When the nurse isn't looking,
I close your fingers
over a strand of the dog's hair.

After All Is Said and Done

For all kind thoughts and all memorials,
we send forth thank-you notes,
rage and love and ashes
in paper boats.

Dissatisfied Life

Taller than the emptied house beside it,
a tree climbs, decade after decade,
quibbling with heaven, waiting
for the cat to pour himself again across the grass,
the daily paper to thunk at sunup in the drive,
the woman to step out in the mornings,
yawning, cursing the rickety stoop.

Snow in Arkansas

Paltry as measles,
it flirts with the ground—
a diva among the awe-struck,
heady with success,
warmly received.
When it comes to town,
schools close in its honor,
drivers sacrifice their cars
before the altar of the white ditch.
Then snow withdraws its troops,
satisfied with the havoc,
the rave reviews,
gone on up north
to be with its people.

The Only Color Blue Should Be

Living in Kansas,
I didn't feel the buffalo through the soles of my shoes,
didn't see in its sky
the only color blue should be,
didn't step into the sunshine
glancing like God's grace off the Missouri.
Yet, held apart from me now
by several states,
Kansas rises in my bones
like a first love
or cancer.

At a Table for Six

Taking respite from her husband's slow dying,
she joins us late.
We babble of war and politics,
horses, children, art.
She keeps a slight distance
as if we were a spectator sport.
Her eyes darken
with the memory of his body, perhaps,
as she laughs at someone's story
volleyed across the white cloth.

Gurney

My daughter lies in the last stage
of her disease.
Making my way
to her hospital room,
I meet a gurney, empty I assume,
until I see the small rise in the covering sheet
where a nose would be.
I know a body is there,
or what is left of one.

I enter her room.
Fighting for my life,
I water the flowers on the windowsill.

Dominion

Such youth, beauty, power—
the first time snow causes a moose to fall
or a house;
the first time it takes a farm,
a town, whole states.
Then the thirst to be exalted
in psalter and paean and ode,
even in prose;
to be lauded for its purity
under a granite moon;
to be feared for its dominion
as far as the crow can see.

Then the slow decline, as sure
as Rome's:
the ruinous warming of the ground,
the vengeful, first spring rains,
the nazi sun,
thinning ranks, skirmishes,
untidy retreats to the north sides of trees.
Then prayers for reinforcements: cold air from Canada,
black ice, a thumping freeze.

Banished from its fiefdoms, the bastions
it so recently pillaged and raped,
snow lies down in rags,
wasted, its color gone bad.
And no one to pay a last respect,
no one to grieve,
no one to mark the bonny fields
of its surrender,

to say one day to visitors
Here. Here is the grave.

Parallel Lives

with a nod to Leonard Cohen and Judy Collins

I've become the guardian of my daughter's jewelry
until her daughters come of age.
These rings, a brooch,
a stone or two
are what they'll touch
as her body turns to lace.

A Young Widower Remembers

As I watched life leave her body,
I thought of country songs we used to dance to,
how the steel guitar slid the music down,
sizzling
to the last note. We lingered,
as hesitant to leave the dance floor,
the harmonica,
each other
as early morning fog to leave a river.

Visiting My Daughter

For weeks
I visited every day,
drawn to that fresh rise,
the blister of her grave.

Things

These things I hold more dearly now:
Breath. Green grass. My husband's
laugh. Chocolate. Hydrangeas. Keys.
Islands off the coast of Maine.
And this dog,
who never tires
of owning me,
who lets me enter every morning
the clear lakes of his eyes.

The Widow Speaks

It's been six months. Everybody is kind
for awhile. I've given away some of his shoes.
I ought to call Goodwill to come for the suits;
none of the children want them, and it's time.

Here's something I've learned: The dead live on in us
their ordinary lives, not knowing they've changed.
If spoken to while drinking their coffee, they may look up.
It's not enough, but something. Try not to complain.

A Woman Speaks of Blue Skies

You and I meet again by chance.
All evening we are giddy,
puffed up like pigeons.
You call the next day
but your words drag their feet.
I hang up the phone. I look out the window.
The sky is blue,
bored as a bone.

Hope

The man waiting for a transplant,
the woman waiting for the chemo to work,
the boy in the projects
waiting for a bike

have all spotted Hope,
that great bird
who may sweep them up,
let them ride between his snowy wings.

It's a long flight.
He tires easily.
Someone will have to be
shaken off.

Suitcases

I'd like not to be a migratory bird,
passion to passion,
saying, too often, goodbye.
I'd like to put these suitcases deep away,
never feel again
their closing sound inside me.

I want to open, summer, winter, summer
the same front door,
feel the same key
dozing in my pocket.

Mother's Day

I water the red impatiens,
the strawflowers and dahlias bordering the lawn.
I lean against the moss-covered bricks
of the house.
I think of the cemetery
where my daughter lies buried young,
orphaned of her children,
incredulous
among those sullen graves.

Ashes

Passing beside the fireplace,
last night's cold fire,
I note a rustling,
as if a wasp were dozing itself awake
inside the morning paper
or a ghost had thought
of something I need to know.

Oaks

When friends came,
bringing food and sympathy,
I asked them to speak of my daughter
in the present tense.

When I visited her grave,
the oak trees,
casting their ferny shadows,
set me straight.

Arkansas

They came in a sizzling 1950s August
to the back door,
three black men raising money
for a black college.
In dark hats and suits,
stepping out of a car
polished like a Steinway,
they made their polite case,
then backed out of the slow drive
raising not a mote of dust.
Past broken tractors and scorched fields,
past farmers cursing God and sprockets,
they floated in that impeccable car,
erect as pharaohs.

Rumors

Once, the house I grew up in
glowed like a Hopper painting,
white paint intact,
its porch light waiting up for me.
Alive now only in my mind,
it is dying—and everything in it—
rumors of shapes
like faces in a photograph
left too long on a sunny table.

Under an Arkansas Sky

CHAPBOOK

2010

Niceties

Whenever I hear, late at night,
Death pilfering my library
and my scotch,
rattling his sleeve against a glass,

I try to engage him pleasantly,
a word or two,
but he will not speak,

snuffing the light,
turning the glass mouth down,
dismissing me.
And in my own house.

My Father Teaches Me to Bat

I miss a pitch
and my father frowns.
I'm nine, ten maybe—
an August afternoon,
he and I standing in the backyard grass.

On another planet, World War II
lumbers near some village
even my father can't pronounce.

No matter. I'm entrenched on this lawn,
in the shadow of my mother's house,
surrounded by fields
that smell like toads.

Under an Arkansas sky
boiled dumb by the heat,
I miss another pitch.

Sitting in a Late-Night Bar, a Woman Recalls

Someone at a far table laughs,
and a boy she'd almost forgotten
ambles a river bank beside her.
Sparrows baptize their song
in the water.

There is a rowboat, two men fishing,
mosquitoes and flies.
The bartender hands her a drink.
The sun eases its way along her shoulders,
melting her blouse.

In Golden Tree Assisted Living, She Protests the Scheme of Things

Once upon a time, not so long ago,
I'd conjure up a man in the evening
and by daybreak he'd come true.
He might not be the one, exactly,
but he would do.

Months ago, I summoned a man to appear
in a Panama hat and a pinstripe suit.
He'd be a good dancer
and make a mean martini.

I have yet to see him.
I guess it's not supposed to be.
I guess this is the way you find out
you're losing your powers.

But who wants to be reminded?
Which may be the reason why
this place and every other like it
goes by some blue-sky, olly-oxen name.

Answering the Question

I'm walking the dog at dusk
and my cat ambles up,
not the one I have now
but another one,
on a younger lawn,

trotting beside me
in the same way
he once lapped his milk,
deliberate, luxuriant,

rubbing against my leg
as if to ask if I remember him,
then slipping into the dark,

knowing, I suspect,
what the dead have always known.

A Day's Work

In this not-yet-sunny kitchen,
I sit in a silence born of the world's patience:
as when a cork is persuaded
from a difficult bottle of wine
while the guests, in anticipation,
lay down their talk—
or when a trolling motor is extinguished
and the fisherman casts his line.

The sun hauls up
its battalions of birds
and the world begins—
peonies in the garden,
the dog to his dish,
a burning car blocking traffic
on I-435 in the eastbound lane—

as I try to describe it
for a woman in Wabunsit, Maine,
or a man leaving Wal-Mart at two a.m.,
hungry for coffee, fries, a canoe willing a lake to rise
to meet it.

INDEX OF POEM TITLES

A native of DeWitt, Arkansas, Jo McDougall is the author of five books and two chapbooks of poetry as well as a memoir. She is associate professor emeritus of English, Pittsburg State University. She has received awards from the DeWitt Wallace/Reader's Digest Foundation, the Academy of American Poets, the Porter Prize Foundation, and fellowships from the MacDowell Colony. A book of new poems is slated for publication by Tavern Books in 2016. She lives in Little Rock.